FlickeringPixels

FlickeringPixels

HOW TECHNOLOGY SHAPES YOUR FAITH

SHANE HIPPS

ZONDERVAN®

ZONDERVAN

Flickering Pixels
Copyright © 2009 by Shane Hipps
Requests for information should be addressed to:
Zondervan, *3900 Sparks Dr. SE, Grand Rapids, Michigan 49546*

ISBN 978-0-310-35037-8 (softcover)

Library of Congress Cataloging-in-Publication Data

Hipps, Shane, 1956-
Flickering pixels : how technology shapes your faith / Shane Hipps.
p. cm.
Some of the material in this book was previously published in The hidden power of electronic culture, 2006.
Includes bibliographical references.
ISBN 978-0-310-29321-7 (hardcover)
1. Christianity and culture. 2. Technology—Influence. 3. Technology—Religious aspects—Christianity. 4. Mass media—Influence. 5. Mass media—Religious aspects—Christianity. I. Title.
BR115.C8H555 2009
261.5'2—dc22 2008045542

All Scripture quotations, unless otherwise indicated, are taken from The Holy Bible, New International Version®, NIV®. Copyright © 1973, 1978, 1984 by Biblica, Inc.® Used by permission of Zondervan. All rights reserved worldwide. www.Zondervan.com. The "NIV" and "New International Version" are trademarks registered in the United States Patent and Trademark Office by Biblica, Inc.®

Scripture quotations marked NASB are taken from the New American Standard Bible®. Copyright © 1960, 1962, 1963, 1968, 1971, 1972, 1973, 1975, 1977, 1995 by The Lockman Foundation. Used by permission. (www.Lockman.org).

Photo on page 76: © 1995 by *The Washington Post*. Photo by Carol Guzy. Reprinted with permission.

Internet addresses (websites, blogs, etc.) and telephone numbers in this book are offered as a resource to you. These are not intended in any way to be or imply an endorsement on the part of Zondervan, nor do we vouch for the content of these sites and numbers for the life of this book.

All rights reserved. No part of this publication may be reproduced, stored in a retrieval system, or transmitted in any form or by any means—electronic, mechanical, photocopy, recording, or any other—except for brief quotations in printed reviews, without the prior permission of the publisher.

Published in association with Yates & Yates, www.yates2.com.

Interior design: Beth Shagene

First printing November 2016 / Printed in the United States of America

For Andrea, my light and love.
For Harper and Hadley, my bliss.

Author's Note

Some of the material in this book was previously published in *The Hidden Power of Electronic Culture: How Media Shapes Faith, the Gospel, and Church* (Zondervan, 2006). That book was aimed at people in church leadership. If you want to explore the topics addressed in this book more deeply, or want to know their implications for leaders and pastors who are trying to form God's people in a changing world, you can go deeper there.

If you've read that book, some of these themes will be familiar. However, in my speaking and travels, I began to hear a growing chorus of voices hungry to know how the connections I was making applied to the rest of life, not just church leadership. I wrote *Flickering Pixels* to apply insights about media and technology to some of the basic issues of our faith and life. While you will find some practical application, the main point of the book is to help you see the world in new ways.

In a sense, this book uses the same color palette but different brush strokes applied to a fresh canvas — I hope you enjoy the painting.

Contents

Hidden Pixels

I instinctively grabbed for the dashboard. The car was careening toward a sudden U-turn curve in the track. I glanced at the driver, expecting him to hit the brakes and avert catastrophe. Instead, he yawned. The car rocketed into the corner as my heart leapt to my throat. Breathing is overrated. The car glided smoothly in and out of the turn as if it had prepared its entire life for that moment. Afterward, the driver apologized for not going faster.

This was part of my "research" for the new ad account I was working on — Porsche cars. The people at Porsche had taken us to a racetrack to develop an appreciation for their product, and apart from nearly soiling my drawers, it worked.

My role as an advertising account planner was to serve as a kind of "consumer anthropologist." That's the sanitized description. More accurately, my task was to hijack your imagination, brand your brain with our logo, and then feed you opinions you thought were your own.

You're welcome.

Much of what I did involved unearthing private, exploitable data from consumers' lives—what we called "The Leverageable Insight." An effective ad tries to tap viewers' most intense and emotional experiences, the trigger for all consumer impulses. My job was to save people from feeling impotent, unattractive, or powerless by offering them a Porsche, which promised to fix those problems.

I'm a slow learner. It took me a few years to realize that I was actually promoting a counterfeit gospel. Before you start judging, you should know I never offered cheap grace—the gospel according to Porsche will set you back between $80,000 and $150,000, depending on how much salvation you need.

Shortly after my awakening, I committed career suicide; I turned my back on a lucrative and enjoyable career and entered seminary. Four years later I accepted a call to serve as the pastor of a church. The emotional and spiritual whiplash was as bad as it sounds, yet the experience led me home.

The conversion began as a result of my own ambition. In an effort to sharpen my ability to manipulate the masses while I was in advertising, I stumbled upon a thinker who had been considered irrelevant for decades. He was an obscure literary professor who studied media and communication in contemporary culture. During the 1960s, his prescient cultural predictions earned him a place on the covers of *Newsweek* and *Life*; it was said his "theory of communication offers nothing less than an explanation of all human culture, past, present, and future."[1] The *New York Herald Tribune* breathlessly declared that he was "the most important thinker since Newton, Darwin, Einstein, Freud, and Pavlov."[2] His name was Marshall McLuhan, and chances are he's the most important thinker you've never heard of.

I began to read McLuhan's *Understanding Media,* which took a wrecking ball to my worldview and became a penetrating alarm that woke me from slumber. I was given a vision of what my profession was doing—and undoing—in our culture, and it wasn't pretty. As I continued reading, I learned something even more important: McLuhan's insights about human culture and communication had profound implications for the Christian faith.

Christianity is fundamentally a communication event. The religion is predicated on God revealing himself to humanity. God has a habit of letting his people know something about his thoughts, feelings, and intentions. God wants to communicate with us, and his media are many: angels, burning bushes, stone tablets, scrolls, donkeys, prophets, mighty voices, still whispers, and shapes traced in the dirt.[3] Any serious study of God is a study of communication, and any effort to understand God is shaped by our understanding—or misunderstanding—of the media and technology we use to communicate.

This book explores the hidden power of media and technology as a way to understand who we are, who we think God is, and how God's unchanging message has changed, is changing, and will change. It's about the way God communicates with us and the way we communicate God to the world. Mostly, though, it's about training our eyes to see things we usually overlook.

Like tiny pixels of light, for example.

Every day we are entranced by a mosaic of flickering pixels. These little dots of light are practically invisible, so minuscule that we often ignore them.

Nevertheless, they change us.

Flickering pixels compose the screens of life, from televisions to cell phones to computers. These screens, regardless of their content, change our brains, alter our lives, and shape our faith, all without our permission or knowledge.

These pixels are only one example of the technologies that shape us. There are more—many more. It is only by shifting our attention that we are able to see them, and in so doing learn to *use them* rather than be used by them.

CHAPTER 1

Mr. No-Depth Perception

In 1991, *Saturday Night Live* introduced America to Mr. No-Depth Perception, played by Kevin Nealon. The character made only one appearance, but the sketch left an indelible mark on my memory. The title tells the story: It's a sketch about an enthusiastic and well-intentioned man who is completely unaware that he cannot perceive depth or distance.

Mr. No-Depth Perception is excited by the prospect of skydiving, imagining how thrilling it must be to "pull the rip cord at just the right moment"—an impossible feat for him to accomplish. Later, he shatters the living room window with his head in a simple attempt to see who is knocking at the door. As his guests, Brenda and Gary, come in and sit down for dinner, Mr. No-Depth Perception turns to his wife and says loudly, "I can't believe Brenda's dating this loser!" Gary, sitting only a few feet away, fidgets awkwardly in his seat. When Mr. No-Depth Perception's wife reprimands him for his insensitivity, he responds by saying, "Oh, relax! He can't hear me way down there!" The sketch goes on like this, but you get the point.

Mr. No-Depth Perception reflects the condition most of us find ourselves in when we try to understand how our culture shapes our faith. We see certain elements of our culture, but we have great difficulty *perceiving* their real importance. For example, we recognize that images and icons are fast displacing words as the dominant communication system of our culture—a trend easily identified by Nike's ability to use its wordless Swoosh icon without losing any brand recognition—but we fail to perceive that the system of visual communication has the capacity to shape and influence faith.

Like Mr. No-Depth Perception, we are often oblivious to the limitations and dangers of our disability, believing instead that we can already see and perceive everything we need. We herald the high virtue of efficiency and effectiveness, eagerly embracing new cultural methods, media, and technologies. We assume our lives and our faith will be stronger, faster, and more relevant, yet we are surprised each time we shatter a window with our heads. All of a sudden life feels more complicated, unmanageable, and dizzying.

One-Eyed Prophets

Humans have a lengthy and ambivalent relationship with technology, something the films *Minority Report, The Matrix,* and *I, Robot* have explored. Such films present apocalyptic visions of social control and the unintended consequences of our obsession with creating ever-more-powerful machines.

In many ways, these movies are contemporary retellings of the dystopian novels of a previous era. George Orwell's *1984* and Aldous Huxley's *A Brave New World*, both written before 1950, are prophetic visions of societies overtaken by technological power. Orwell's novel introduces us to the all-seeing, always-watching "Big Brother" and warns of a dark future where conformity is guaranteed by invasive and controlling technology. In contrast, *A Brave New World* describes a seductive, seemingly utopian future in which technological promise is the succulent but poisoned apple that leads to humanity's downfall.

In nineteenth-century England, a group of disgruntled textile artisans known as the Luddites destroyed the machinery in wool and cotton mills to protest the dehumanizing technological advances of the Industrial Revolution.

In our time, the Amish maintain an equally radical, albeit less violent, rejection of certain technologies. A prohibition on automobiles and electricity is central to the corporate practice of the Amish faith. While such a stance might appear to be an arbitrary time freeze, it is deeply informed by this community's theology of technology.

Even these warnings about the dangers of technology are not the earliest. Several thousand years ago, a nomadic culture wandering in the Sinai desert was warned about the technology of images. The Hebrew people tell the story of a God named Yahweh who issued ten moral teachings, one of which explicitly prohibits using images as a medium for worship: "You shall not make for yourself graven images."[1] There is no explanation beyond this, but for some reason this God is concerned about the things we use to communicate and make meaning. In fact, his concern is so strong that the warning comes in second on his top-ten list.

Not long after this, in another part of the world, a Greek philosopher named Plato retells a story about Socrates teaching one of his pupils. In Socrates' story, there are two Egyptian gods: a king named Thamus and an inventor named Theuth, who was known to have invented, among other things, geometry, arithmetic, astronomy, and writing. As Socrates tells it:

> Now the king of all Egypt at that time was the god Thamus ... To him came Theuth to show his inventions, saying that they ought to be imparted to the other Egyptians ... When it came to writing, Theuth declared, "... I have discovered a sure receipt for memory and wisdom." To this, Thamus replied, "... you have attributed to it quite the opposite of its real function. Those who acquire it will cease to exercise their memory and become forgetful ... What you have discovered is a receipt for recollection, not for memory. And as for wisdom, your pupils will have the reputation for it without the reality: they will receive a quantity of information without proper instruction ... And because they are filled with the conceit of wisdom instead of real wisdom they will be a burden to society.[2]

In his book *Technopoly,* cultural critic Neil Postman employs the Thamus story to illustrate an important point. King Thamus, who is opposed to writing, and Theuth, who heralds the promise of writing, are both "one-eyed prophets," each with the opposite eye closed.[3] They each speak a measure of truth while simultaneously conveying a subtle error. Thamus has a point: Writing does erode memory, and while writing can provide new knowledge, it's not the same as wisdom.

A friend recently said to me, "I had the most amazing insight about my spiritual life this morning. It was ... basically, like ... uh ... let me get my journal, I wrote it down." He then read his insight to me, periodically interrupting his own reading to enjoy his discovery all over again—"Oh yeah, *that's* what it was!" He couldn't remember the meaning or specifics of his spiritual breakthrough from just four hours earlier. When he was finished reading, he reported, "Since I've started writing this stuff down, I can't remember anything without my journal."

The erosion of memory is, in fact, a downside of the invention of writing; however, there is also an upside that Thamus failed to perceive. Reading and writing have an incredible capacity to expand consciousness and advance the common good. Consider the Reformation, which challenged the corruption and abuse of the medieval Catholic church. This would not have happened without a rise in literacy among the masses. Their ability to see directly for themselves what Scripture said is what gave traction and support to Martin Luther's cause. Or consider the fact that free democratic forms of government have a tendency to take root and thrive in cultures with high literacy rates. Democracies demand that citizens have access to information in order to make informed decisions. Literacy provides this on a scale that a purely oral culture does not.

We need both eyes open if we are going to perceive the multitude of subtle forces that shape our lives. Technology both gives and takes away, and each new medium introduced into our lives must be evaluated. As Postman put it, our culture is teeming with "throngs of zealous Theuths, one-eyed prophets who see only what new technologies can do and are incapable of imagining what they will *undo*."[4]

On the road ahead, we will see what it means to keep both eyes open.

CHAPTER 2

The Magic Eye

Recently, I was talking to a guy who was trying to create new and innovative ways to spread the gospel message, and what he'd come up with was a Christian-themed video game. "We're just trying to give a new generation a chance to connect with Jesus," he said. "It's not that the truth and content change, but the mediums have to change." This is the North Star by which the vast majority of Christians have navigated the perpetual changes in culture.

The methods always change, but the message stays the same.

The point is simple enough. The forms of Christianity must change as people change—if they didn't we'd all have to learn Hebrew, Greek, and Aramaic in order to read the Bible. A Bible translation is actually a new medium—the medium of a different language. We take our countless Bible translations for granted, but this was a bitter point of contention at various points in church history. The church has a history and habit of resisting methodological changes.

The same debate is alive today. Just pick a different medium. In the end, whether we translate the Bible into another language or use television to broadcast a preacher's message, these innovations dramatically extend the reach of the gospel. Therefore, it is commonly assumed that as long as we protect the unchanging *message* of the gospel, the *method* of communicating doesn't much matter.

After all, everyone knows that our media are merely tools — they are neither good nor bad, but simply neutral conduits or pipelines to channel information. In a sense, media are like the plumbing of a house, carrying water from one place to the next. The pipes don't matter much unless they spring a leak.

The logic is pretty straightforward. Unfortunately, that doesn't make it true.

The belief that media are neutral tools is only half right. Marshall McLuhan, the oracle of the electronic age, reveals the error of this assumption when he says that "the medium is the message." If the first truth is that our methods necessarily change, the second truth is that whenever our methods change, the message automatically changes along with them. You can't change methods without changing your message — they're inseparable.

McLuhan elaborates, writing, "Our conventional response to all media, namely that it is how they are used that counts, is the numb stance of the technological idiot. For the 'content' of a medium is like the juicy piece of meat carried by the burglar to distract the watchdog of the mind."[1] In another passage he exaggerates to state the matter even more forcefully: "The content or message of any particular medium has about as much importance as the stenciling on the casing of an atomic bomb."[2]

In other words, the various media through which we acquire information are not neutral. Instead, they have the power to shape us, regardless of content, and we cannot evaluate them based solely on their content. McLuhan challenges the notion that if a medium dispenses violence or sex, it is bad, but if it dispenses Christian content, it is good. A televised sermon redeems the medium of television. But when MTV depicts explicit sexuality and public drunkenness, the medium of TV is poisoned.

These assumptions ignore the fact that the television image itself shapes us. When we watch television, we are oblivious to the medium itself. The flickering mosaic of pixilated light washes over us, bypassing our conscious awareness. Instead, we sit hypnotized by the program —the content—which has gripped our attention, unaware of the ways in which the television, regardless of its content, is repatterning the neural pathways in our brain and reducing our capacity for abstract thought.

The screen itself is part of the message.

Just as Dorothy and her companions missed the man behind the curtain in *The Wizard of Oz*, we often fail to notice the hidden power of media. Most of us point and stare at the giant wizard-head wreathed in flame, quite unaware that it is only a trick of the brain—the magician's sleight of hand as he slips the watch from our wrist.

Wake Up, Neo

In the first *Matrix* film, there is a pivotal scene in which Neo, the main character, is about to get an answer to the question that has been driving him: "What is the matrix?" Morpheus, the prophetic guide, has taken Neo into a secret room. Neo anxiously awaits the big revelation. But something strange happens that diverts his attention. To Neo's right is a cracked mirror, which reflects a fractured image of him. As Neo looks at the mirror, the cracks suddenly begin to recede and bleed together, making the mirror whole again. Neo's reflection is no longer fractured, and he is startled. The move from a cracked mirror to a whole one foreshadows the clarity Neo is about to get about the technology that has imprisoned him.

Doing a double take, Neo asks if this is a dream. He begins to study the mirror rather than his reflection. He reaches out to touch it, but at the point of contact it bends and bows like liquid mercury, then snaps plumb again around his fingers. Neo quickly recoils from this strange medium, but a portion of the mysterious mirror adheres to his fingers and rapidly multiplies until it begins to consume him. Immediately, the film cuts to Neo trapped in an incubation pod, struggling to escape. From here he is born into the "real world," and the whole story turns in a new direction. There is no going back.

In this case the mirror is a metaphor for the technological world of the Matrix. At first the mirror appears rather harmless, but suddenly, it takes on a life of its own. In the same way, the world the humans created in the film was initially benign but eventually took on a life of its own and enslaved the whole human race.

When Neo studies the medium of the mirror instead of being distracted by his reflection—its content—he is freed from the prison of his mind; it is only when he observes the medium apart from its content that he perceives its true power. With this discovery, he is awakened from his numbness and slumber. So are we.

The Magic Eye

In the late '90s a trend swept the nation, at least for about fifteen minutes. In malls across America, Magic Eye posters bloomed like wildflowers. These stereograms were two-dimensional images that gave the illusion of three dimensions. On the surface, the posters appeared to be meaningless, repetitive patterns of shapes, letters, or colors; but each poster contained a hidden message or image. By focusing just beyond the

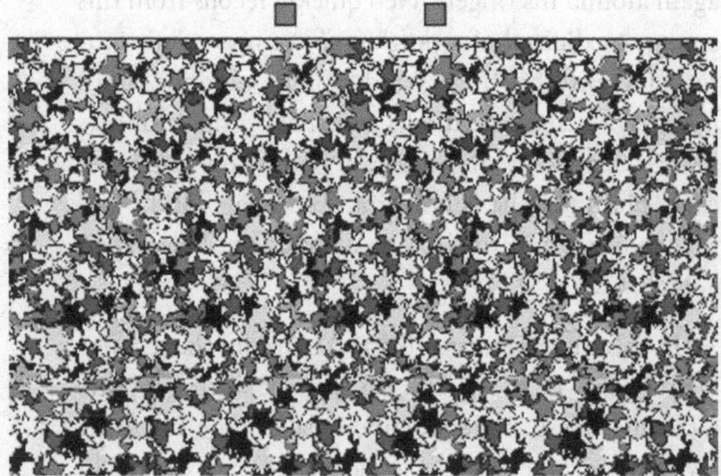

surface of the poster, a trained viewer could witness the magic appearance of an image that seemed to leap out into space.

If you can't see this on your own, try this: Hold the image up to your nose until it's blurry. Look beyond the photo into the distance. Slowly move the image away until the two squares above the image become three. If you see four squares you haven't gone far enough. If you see one or two squares, try it again.

When you see three squares, the image will appear. The dimension gets deeper the farther away you are from it.[3]

Can you see the hidden message below?

```
lude the as include the as include the as include the as include the as include
ute a right minute a right minute a right minute a right minute a right minute
wn year left down year left down year left down year left down year left down y
mpiler error compiler error compiler error compiler error compiler error compil
econd month i second month i second month i second month i second month i secon
using face her using face her using face her using face her using face her usin
they stop tart they stop tart the stop start the stop start the stop start the
it at wasting pit at wasting pit a wasting spit a wasting spit a wasting spit a
an hast your lean hast your lean has your clean has your clean has your clean h
ead cars time lead cars time lead car time plead car time plead car time plead
 i my go bottom i my go bottom i my go bottom i my go bottom i my go bottom i m
get over frogs get over frogs get over frogs get over frog get hover frog get h
n a pore old and a pore old and a pore old and a pore old an a spore old an a s
rm life rink farm life rink farm life rink farm life rink far life drink far li
server my date server my date server my date server my date server my date serv
back ever fort back ever fort back ever fort back ever fort back ever fort back
 this is filler this is filler this is filler this is filler this is filler thi
up into out of up into out of up into out of up into out of up into out of up i
l never act will never act will never act will never act will never act will ne
lly in the totally in the totally in the totally in the totally in the totally
em a look problem a look problem a look problem a look problem a look problem a
anyone is hide anyone is hide anyone is hide anyone is hide anyone is hide anyo
and distribute and distribute and distribute and distribute and distribute and
```

These images can be maddening to look for. The muscles of the eyes aren't trained to look beyond the page, and many a viewer has walked away in frustration. But if you stick with it long enough and finally see the hidden image, your eyes will always remember how to do it. The more you do it, the more the image stabilizes, and each time you look it comes into focus more quickly.

Spoiler alert: If you can't see the hidden images, here they are. The first stereogram reveals the image of Saturn. The second one offers a subtle message. When your eyes adjust, two little sentences begin to hover above the scrambled sea of letters—"stop wasting your time" and "get a life."

Magic Eye posters and our media have something in common. In order for their hidden messages to be rightly perceived, both need to be viewed in an unconventional way. We need to train our eyes to focus beyond the surface of our technologies. When we do, our familiar world begins to look disconcertingly strange. With practice, however, our eyes will focus more easily, and we'll be that much closer to seeing things as they are.

CHAPTER 3

Stretch Armstrong

I remember vividly an action figure I had when I was little called Stretch Armstrong—I could pull his arms and legs almost all the way across the living room without snapping them, and when I let go, they'd return gently to their original position. Media and technology are kind of like Stretch Armstrong: They extend our reach—our words, sounds, images, and even our selves—beyond our normal limits.

Our culture most often uses the word *media* in reference to "The Media"—that voyeuristic and omnipresent beast comprised of countless channels, celebrity rags, radio stations, and newspapers that invades our imagination and insatiably devours everything in its path. That definition, however, is too limited. McLuhan offers a more complete understanding of the term, stating that a medium is anything that stretches, extends, or amplifies some human capacity.[1]

In this expanded definition, media may extend a part of our body, one or more of our senses, some function of our mental processes, or some social process. For example, the invention of the wheel is an extension of our body in that it amplifies the function of the foot. The telephone extends and amplifies the voice and the ear. Eyeglasses extend the focusing ability of the eye. Weapons, such as guns or knives, are extensions of our teeth and our fists. Smoke detectors extend our sense of smell and also amplify our feeling of security. Even a method of organizing information, such as an outline, is a medium because it extends the mind's ability to comprehend and recall complex topics.

Communications technologies such as the telegraph, cell phones, email, books, and even the spoken word are also media. In fact, by this definition all human creations or cultural artifacts are a medium of one kind or another — from cars and clothing to clocks and credit cards. The more we invent and extend ourselves, Stretch Armstrong-style, the more the world changes. As the world shrinks, we witness the violent collision of previously distant cultures. McLuhan termed this reality the "Global Village." It is changing how we live as humans, as well as how we practice faith and the ways we imagine God.

The Problem of Narcissus

Greek mythological hero Narcissus was blessed by the gods with supernatural good looks. All the women of the world adored him, but he never returned their love. Over time, the maidens grew angry and asked the gods to curse Narcissus with the pain of unrequited love. The gods listened.

Deep in the woods they created a pool of pure, silver water. One day, Narcissus stumbled upon the pool, exhausted and thirsty from a day of hunting. Leaning over to drink, he saw his own image mirrored in the water, but he mistook it for a beautiful water spirit living in the pool. As he gazed at those bright eyes, curled locks of hair, and healthy glow, he fell in love.

But when he leaned forward to kiss the fair face, it fled at the moment of contact. In time it would return, and Narcissus became enamored once more. He was so taken by the image in the water that he lost all thought of food or rest. Soon, Narcissus began to starve, but the pain of hunger could not overpower the stunning beauty that enraptured him. Eventually, he withered away and died.

The traditional interpretation of this story is that Narcissus fell in love with himself; it was the Greek warning against excessive self-love. Sigmund Freud later derived the term *narcissism* from this myth as a way to describe the psychological neurosis of extreme selfishness and self-interest. McLuhan also used this story to illustrate an important point—one that was different from Freud's.

The chief error of Narcissus was not that he fell in love with himself but rather that he failed to *recognize* himself in the water's reflection. Narcissus became "numb" to his own extended image in the low-tech medium of a water mirror. He could not perceive that the image was simply an extension of himself, and so he gave the image power to harm and ultimately kill. If Narcissus had understood that the water was simply a mirror reflecting his own face, the mirror's power would have been dispelled, and Narcissus could have gained control over it. Narcissus—derived from the Greek word *narcosis,* which means "numbness"—became enslaved to his own image. When we fail to perceive that the things we create are extensions of ourselves, the created things take on god-like characteristics and we become their servants.[2]

The Solution of Perseus

Another Greek myth offers a helpful solution to the problem of Narcissus. This myth tells of a young man named Perseus, a son of the god Zeus. In the land where Perseus grew up, a horrifying monster named Medusa was on a rampage; everyone who looked directly into her eyes was immediately turned to stone. Perseus volunteered to destroy her.

As Perseus set out for Medusa's lair, the gods gave him a highly polished shield for protection. When Perseus arrived, Medusa was sleeping. He approached quietly, being cautious never to look directly at her. Rather than proceeding with his eyes closed, he used his bright shield as a guiding mirror, keeping his eyes fixed on the reflection of Medusa. Suddenly, she awoke with a hiss and glared at Perseus, but because he saw only her reflection in his shield, her gaze had no effect. Immediately, Perseus struck with his sword, shearing off her head. Upon his return, Perseus offered Medusa's head as a gift to the king, and there was peace in the land.

In both of these myths, the plot hinges on the low-tech medium of a mirror. For Narcissus, the pool mirror was a mysterious and powerful medium he could not understand. He was distracted by the content—his own reflection—and it gained power over him, leading to his death. Perseus, on the other hand, was aware that the mirror was an extension of himself that he could control. This understanding allowed him to survive an ordeal that had claimed the lives of countless others. In the same way, when we remember that technology is simply an extension of ourselves, it takes much of the power away from the medium and returns it to us.

This is a human experience not consigned to obscure Greek myths. I was having lunch with a friend recently and as we chatted, his ringing cell phone interrupted nearly every other sentence. "Sorry, I have to get this," he would say. Each time I would wait, and each time he would apologize. The last time it rang he said, with a sense of resignation and exhaustion, "I am a total slave to my cell phone." When we realize that a cell phone is merely an extension of ourselves, this statement makes as much sense as saying, "I am a slave to my ears or my voice"—the very parts of ourselves that the cell phone extends.

4D Vision

Mr. No-Depth Perception saw the world in two dimensions, and many of us share his plight when it comes to technology and culture. By understanding that media are extensions of ourselves, we begin to develop depth to our perception and see an additional dimension.

This is quite useful, but it is still insufficient. There are actually four dimensions to all media.[3]

The first we have discussed—the Stretch Armstrong dimension of amplification or extension. The second dimension is that every new medium makes an older technology irrelevant or obsolete. To make something irrelevant or obsolete, however, does not make it disappear; it simply changes the function of the older artifact. For example, the automobile made the horse and buggy obsolete, but the horse-drawn carriage has not disappeared. It has simply changed its function from an essential work vehicle to a way for tourists to explore Central Park.

The third dimension borrows from the truth that there is nothing new under the sun. In other words, every new medium retrieves some experience or medium from the past. For example, the Internet retrieves the telegraph. Painkiller drugs attempt to retrieve the comfort of a mother's womb. The surveillance camera, which is designed for protection, retrieves the ancient and medieval city wall, which fended off barbarian invasions.

The fourth dimension is the most difficult to see. It is the dark dimension. Every medium, when pushed to an extreme, will reverse on itself, revealing unintended consequences. For example, the car was invented to increase the speed of our transportation, but having too many cars on the highway at once results in traffic jams or even injury and death. The Internet was designed to make information more easily accessible, thereby reducing ignorance. But too much information or the wrong kind of information reverses into overwhelming the seeker, leading to greater confusion rather than clarity. It breeds misunderstanding rather than wisdom.

By understanding what thing from the past a medium retrieves, we are better to anticipate its reversal. For example, if surveillance cameras retrieve the ability of the medieval city wall to protect citizens, what did the city wall reverse into? Well, when fires erupted in ancient cities, which they often did, the walls created a new and unintended vulnerability. The walls functioned like a prison, trapping the city's residents inside where the danger was. In the same way, surveillance cameras, when there are too many that see too far, reverse into an invasion of privacy. This invasion of privacy creates an unintended but very real vulnerability. It functions like a prison in which your every move is voyeuristically monitored and recorded.

Has technology in your life ever reversed? What would it look like for your camera, your cell phone, or even the book you're reading right now to reverse?

CHAPTER 4

Dyslexia and Deception

When my daughter Harper was two, we started singing the ABC song together. In the process we introduced her to one of the most powerful technologies the world has ever known. It's the one you are consuming right now: the technology of letters, the invention of writing. In a way, teaching her how to read is actually teaching her brain to do something completely unnatural. The skills of walking and talking arrived intuitively over time, but reading and writing forced her brain to operate in a way that was not innate. She had to learn to compress reality into line after line of strange shapes arranged in sequence. Such a technology takes work to master and, when mastered, completely transforms our consciousness.

I don't take the medium of writing for granted. As a second grader, I remember being tortured by in-class reading tests. I had to use every last brain cell to decipher the words and sentences on the page. After straining through the first couple of sentences, I would inevitably notice that the two kids on either side had already flipped to the next page while I was still stuck on the first paragraph.

A panic would set in. I started turning the page whenever they did, so I wouldn't look dumb or slow. It seemed like a good plan at the time. Of course, we were often quizzed on the material we had just read (or in my case not read), and, needless to say, I did not score well. Fortunately, in short order my teachers and parents caught on. I was eventually tested for learning disabilities and diagnosed with dyslexia — a condition often caricatured as reading words backward. My dyslexia is a bit more subtle; every time I look at the printed page, I feel like I've just walked out of a dark movie theater into the bright light of day. It takes time for my eyes to adjust and begin cobbling together the letters on the page into something that makes sense.

My difficulties with reading and writing didn't just affect my schoolwork. Dyslexia actually makes my brain function differently than the brains of others. In those early diagnostic tests, I also scored very low on both visual perception and the ability to organize information or objects. This is common for kids who have dyslexia. Reading and writing demand the visual organization of objects, in this case, letters.

That meant that in addition to my reading difficulties, my desk at school was a hopeless mess, a black hole for most of my homework assignments. In contrast, those without difficulty reading had no trouble with visual perception and could organize information and objects with ease. Whether they chose to be organized was a different matter—the point is they had a competence that I did not.

At the same time, compared to normal readers I scored extremely high in the area of short-term memory. This phenomenon is not uncommon among children with dyslexia or other reading problems.

The explanation is quite simple: Like a blind person who develops acute hearing for survival, my brain compensated for my visual deficits by enhancing memory, specifically auditory memory. Because I could barely access information through the visual act of reading, I depended upon retaining what the teacher said for my learning. Incidentally, as I have become more fluent in the world of literacy, my organizational skills have improved and my short-term memory has diminished. My wife can attest to this fact.

The fact that I didn't read or write much made me a very different thinker—a different person, actually. What was true for me on an individual level is true on a cultural level, too. The broad introduction of literacy into an entire culture completely alters the way that culture thinks. Writing restructures the worldview of entire civilizations.

We Become What We Behold

We're told that we are what we eat. With some exceptions, when most of us eat a lot of fatty foods, we get fat. But there is one expression that's true for everyone—we become what we behold.[1] That is to say, our thinking patterns actually mirror the things we use to think with.

Most of us are aware of some basic cultural differences that exist between cultures of the East and the West, but what may surprise us is that many of these differences are a direct result of something as simple as the alphabet.

The Chinese use a pictographic or ideographic alphabet, while the West uses a phonetic alphabet. In Chinese, a single character represents an entire word or concept and often looks a bit like the thing it describes. For example, see if you can guess what the following Chinese character represents:

This character actually translates as "woman." And you can see the hints of a human form. But beyond simply depicting the shape of a stick figure, this particular character traces the subtle attributes of feminine energy. You can see beauty, curves, and movement in the character—almost like it's dancing. This is a visual art form, not just a writing system.

In contrast, our phonetic alphabet uses symbols that correspond to a meaningless "phoneme," or vocal sound, rather than an idea or object. The symbol *t* corresponds to the sound /t/ at the beginning of the word *top*. Taken by itself, /t/ is meaningless. Yet when these symbols are arranged sequentially to re-create the sound of the spoken words, they gain meaning. Unlike Chinese, the English word *woman* looks nothing like a woman; it merely indicates and creates the sound of the word.

The phonetic alphabet requires letters be organized in linear sequence in order to generate meaning. The symbols *a, o, m, w,* and *n* don't mean anything until they are arranged as *w-o-m-a-n*. By contrast a single Chinese symbol can stand alone and carry full meaning. In a basic sense, the phonetic alphabet is linear, sequential, and abstract; the Chinese alphabet is holistic, intuitive, and more concrete.

Because we become what we behold, the East and the West began thinking in ways that mirror their respective alphabets. The Western way of thinking, introduced by the Greeks who perfected the phonetic alphabet,[2] is based on something called a *syllogism*. A syllogism is simply a linear, sequential thought pattern. Books like this one are full of them. But here's a simple example:

All humans have a brain.

All men are human.

Therefore, all men have a brain.

You may take issue with the conclusion of this syllogism, but the point is that it mirrors the linear, sequential form of the Western alphabet.

This is different from the way Eastern thought generally works. For example, Eastern philosophy is basically nonlinear and holistic. There is a simple image that shows this approach to thinking called the *yin-yang*.

The image represents the unity of opposites or the oneness of polarities—dark and light, heaven and earth, good and evil, feminine and masculine. These are all opposing things that also somehow exist as an indivisible and complementary whole. This way of thinking mirrors the holistic, intuitive characters that make up the Eastern alphabet.

The tools we use to think actually *shape* the way we think. The same applies to our faith as well.

The Efficient Gospel

The printing press had been in existence in China for nearly 800 years prior to its European debut in the 1400s, and yet it had none of the same liberating intellectual effects it had in the West.[3] The simple explanation is efficiency. The Chinese language just wasn't very efficient. Because each symbol in the Chinese language represents an entire word or idea, a dizzying number of characters are required for communication. In fact, that number could be equal to the number of words in the language—the Chinese dictionary has more than 80,000 characters and is still growing.[4] The idea of using the printing press for mass communication in China made about as much sense as creating a computer keyboard with 80,000 keys.

In this sense, the most breathtaking achievement of the phonetic alphabet is its remarkable efficiency—only twenty-six symbols are needed for endless communication. An infinite number of thoughts can be expressed simply by arranging and rearranging these twenty-six shapes. The invention of the phonetic alphabet helped shape Western thought, but its true force became apparent only after it was channeled through the medium of print.

In the fifteenth century, Johannes Gutenberg found an innovative use for a wine press, and the modern age of the printing press was born. Three media ingredients —paper, printing, and the alphabet—combined to ignite an explosion of nuclear proportions. In Gutenberg's printing press, the phonetic alphabet was given a megaphone to amplify its reach. Printing made writing perfectly uniform and infinitely repeatable. For over four centuries, the printing press made the printed word the standard way of communicating and learning in the Western world.

The printing press was the first assembly line, the archetype for nearly every kind of mechanization that followed.[5] This efficient, linear, sequential form of visual organization helped make possible the Industrial Revolution and the subsequent methods of mass production used to make everything from minivans to milkshakes.

The linear arrangement of pews in churches didn't

exist before the printing press. The medieval church didn't have pews—just a wide-open space for standing. After the printing press, church seating started to mirror the page of a book.

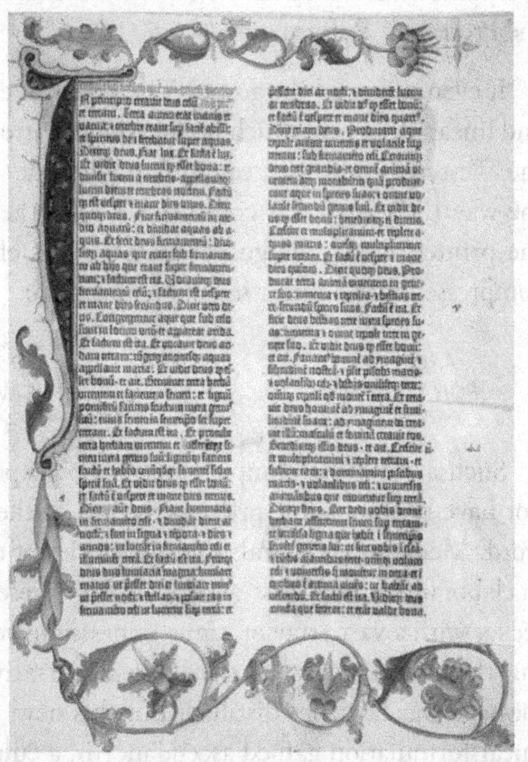

The impact of the printed medium is nearly endless. It not only led to a restructuring of physical space, it restructured our imagination and beliefs as well. This mass production placed information into the hands of everyone, which created the conditions that launched the Protestant Reformation.[6]

It even reshaped the gospel. The values of efficiency and linear sequence, which became more entrenched in the Western world with each passing decade, changed the way the gospel was conceived. Under the force of the printed word, the gospel message was efficiently compressed into a linear sequential formula:

APOLOGIZE FOR YOUR SINS + *BELIEVE JESUS* = *GO TO HEAVEN*

Such a stunning compression of the gospel would not have been possible prior to the age of the printed word. Medieval cathedrals told the stories of the Bible in elaborate stained-glass windows. They presented the seeker with a vast array of vague impressions representing the grand sweep of the biblical narrative—the message was far from distilled. But this new, abstract, linear formulation gained ascendancy in a culture that increasingly communicated via the abstract, linear nature of the printed word. This incredible reduction and synthesis of the gospel eventually became a cornerstone for the modern evangelical expression of faith.

We become what we behold.

Beware of Your Feelings

The apostle Paul was a highly literate man, and his letters reflect the kind of abstract if/then reasoning characteristic of a highly literate, educated mind. During the Middle Ages, before the invention of the printing press, the letters of Paul were seldom taught because their complex messages could not be captured in stained-glass scenes or illustrated prayer books. As a medium, stained glass windows are only able to represent iconic stories, like those found in the Gospels—Jesus healed, wept, ate, died, and rose again. But they are hard-pressed to articulate the dense theological reasoning of Paul's letters.

The printing press not only resuscitated the letters of Paul, it also helped cultivate the reasoning skills necessary in culture to comprehend his message. This is one reason why Martin Luther's rediscovery of Paul's letters resonated with print culture in a way it couldn't have before that point.

Problems arose, however, when linear reasoning was pushed to the extreme. The medium reversed, as all media eventually do when overextended. Linear reasoning became the primary means of understanding and propagating faith. This led to a belief that the gospel could be established and received *only* through reason and fact. Printing makes us prefer cognitive modes of processing while at the same time atrophying our appreciation for mysticism, intuition, and emotion. It can even make us suspicious or fearful of feelings, especially as they interact with our "logical" faith.

The print age preference for linear reasoning and suspicion of feelings is well illustrated by "The Four Spiritual Laws," an evangelistic tract by the late Bill Bright. In this pamphlet, Bright laid out the syllogism of four abstract propositions one must believe in order to be saved. The doctrines must be accepted through reason. Then, in your mind, you move Jesus from the category of a "Man" to the category of "God."

Once you've done this, Bright issues a stark warning under the heading "Do Not Depend on Feelings." What follows is a well-known train diagram and subsequent explanation. (Notice that the linear, sequential arrangement of the diagram directly mirrors the form of the printed word.)

According to Bright, the train will run with or without a caboose; however, it would be useless to attempt to pull the train with the caboose. In the same way, as Christians we do not depend on feelings or emotions, but we place our reasoned trust in God's promises given to us in his printed Word.[7]

This is pretty typical of the print mind. The exaltation of reason is the great legacy of the print age. Printing helped fund the rapid acceleration of higher-order thinking and intellectual development. What an extraordinary gift that was to us. However, when it reverses, the print mind tends to devalue the heart. Emotions are seen as pesky little distractions that get in the way of good reasoning. The consequence is that people are reduced to merely cognitive, rational beings. The problem is, we are not *just* rational beings. The Psalms reveal a very different picture. These are the poems of the heart, and they show us that the emotional life is integral to our very being and life with God (Psalms 6, 13, 102, 103, etc.).

But there is another reason that the demotion of emotions is a problem: Our emotions are powerful governors of behavior and are not easily dismissed or denied. Trying to ignore an emotion by putting it at the back of the train doesn't actually work. Eventually, it will halt the train and start pulling in the other direction. Bury an emotion, and it often resurrects in the form of something more meddlesome. It might masquerade as something else, like an addiction to food, sex, abusive relationships, or power. The heart does not take kindly to being ignored or restrained.

But perhaps the most damaging effect of suppressing the heart is that it deadens desire. That deep longing for life, love, and God fades. Instead, we come to expect less from life. We acquire the bland taste of a domesticated god who resides somewhere in our head. But our head is not home for the divine. The head helps us understand the divine from a safe distance. This is a powerful and valuable enterprise to be sure, but there is a difference between knowing *about* God and knowing God.

Knowing God comes through direct experience. This experience blooms in a wide-open heart where desire burns fiercely and freely. In this way, desire is the path to experiencing God. Desire in all its forms. Even our dark desires, the ones we're most fearful and ashamed of, the ones we call sin. Even those desires are merely disfigured drives searching for the divine in counterfeit form. If we pay attention to them, own them, and push beneath them by peeling back layer upon layer of desire, we eventually find our Original Desire—the deepest longing that leads us home.

CHAPTER 5

Subliminal Messages

Let's get back to Kevin Nealon, but this time we'll look at another one of his *Saturday Night Live* characters —Mr. Subliminal. As before, the name tells the story: Mr. Subliminal has a unique power to persuade and manipulate people by whispering subliminal messages under his breath, frequently conveying the opposite of his explicit message. In one sketch Mr. Subliminal is sitting at a bar, talking with the bartender:

Mr. Subliminal: A beer, please.

Bartender: All right, sir, here's your beer.

Mr. Subliminal: Thanks, partner (*on the house).* That was quick (*on the house)*. What do I owe you?

Bartender: Uh, forget about it. On the house!

Mr. Subliminal: Oh? Thank you very much! Hey, you know something (*free cash)*? This is a real classy place (*free cash).* First time I've been here.

Bartender: Oh, I'm glad you like it. I've been working here for years.

Mr. Subliminal: Oh, no kidding (*free cash)*? That's great!

Bartender: [opens cash register and drops cash on the counter] Here ya go.

Mr. Subliminal: What's this for?

Bartender: It's free cash; take it.

Mr. Subliminal: No, really (*your wallet*). I can't take this cash (*your wallet*). I mean, what would I do with it?

Bartender: Well, don't be ridiculous! [drops his wallet on the counter] Here, take my wallet—you can put it in there!

Mr. Subliminal: Well, okay, if you insist!

Mr. Subliminal has the enviable talent of using subliminal messages to control people without their knowledge, and the printed word can act in a similar way. Regardless of what is being communicated, the printed word whispers subliminal messages (*you're an individual)* as we read. The subject matter *(remain objective)* could be anything. Regardless of the content, we are *(think abstractly)* powerfully shaped by the form (*think rationally)* of the words alone.

"I" Is for Individual

I had a much better memory before I could read well. In fact, many people living in oral cultures have remarkable memories. Such a capacity is necessary for retaining the tribal narratives which give meaning and identity. Because oral cultures have no way to store information or knowledge outside of the mind, once they learn something, they depend upon the community to retain it. Mostly this is done through repetition—telling and retelling stories in an oral tradition that spans many generations.

The invention of writing gave people the luxury of thinking apart from the tribe without the concern of those thoughts disappearing. As reading and writing became available to more and more people, the community was no longer needed to retain teachings, traditions, or identity. And because the tasks of reading and writing often encourage being alone, tribes and communities can be fractured as people spend greater amounts of time in private. This isolation creates the conditions necessary for a strong sense of individualism to emerge. In pre-literate societies, a person's identity is bound to the tribe; the notion of the individual has little importance. However, the *technology* of writing, regardless of *content*, weakens and even destroys tribal bonds and profoundly amplifies the value of the individual.[1]

As a consequence for Christians, certain spiritual disciplines become increasingly preferred, such as the so-called "quiet time," which includes time alone for reading Scripture, solitary prayer, and journaling—all individual and private practices. By contrast, people in oral cultures can find it difficult to gain distance from others or themselves. This can lead to a spirituality that is almost entirely communal in character. During the Medieval period, paper supplies disappeared and the West was returned mostly to an oral culture. As a result, the masses expressed spirituality almost exclusively through the communal ritual of the Eucharist.

The shift from the tribe or community to the individual changed the way the church thought about the gospel. The modern age conceived of a gospel that matters primarily for the individual. The gospel was reduced to forgiveness as a transaction, a concern for personal morality, and the intellectual pursuit of doctrinal precision. In this view, the Bible became little more than a personal handbook for moral living and right thinking. On balance, the technology of printing has helped erode the communal nature of faith.

Community in the print age has been understood primarily as a collection of discrete individuals working concurrently on their personal relationships with Jesus. The church became a thousand points of light and lost sight of itself as the body of Christ—a living, breathing entity whose power is derived from the whole, not the sum of its parts. Under the influence of the print age, our experience of faith gradually moves from something that is personal to something private.

Growing Apart

It may shock you to learn that my wife and I have been known to disagree from time to time. It's usually pretty harmless, but sometimes things get heated. When the tension is so high that we're only hurting each other, we try to call a time-out and get some space to let our emotions cool. During those times, I have occasionally written down my thoughts and feelings. I find that this journaling is a powerful way to get distance from the situation and myself, which gives me much needed perspective.

In oral cultures, where it can be difficult to separate one's self from one's ideas or feelings, this kind of distancing and cooling rarely emerges. Western psychologists would diagnose an oral culture as emotionally "enmeshed." Writing gives people the luxury to act without reacting. It separates the knower from the known, thereby allowing us to stand outside our thoughts and feelings and observe them apart from ourselves in time and space.

This type of detachment can help produce a measure of objectivity, intellectual clarity, perspective, and precision. This is the sort of distance that writers need to edit their work, or doctors need to review their surgical techniques. However, as the age of print entrenched itself in the West, an unintended consequence of such distance emerged: We began to believe that our objectivity was absolute. As a result, our theological assumptions began to change for the worse and a reversal emerged.

We started reading Scripture under the illusion we could know God's mind with unbiased clarity of vision. We presumed the Bible presented an objective set of propositions that everyone would discover with proper time and training. What emerged from this new style of reading and relating to God was a theological and evangelical arrogance.

In reality, our subjective experience is inescapable. Whether I acknowledge it or not, I read the Bible through the lenses of a privileged white American male who was raised in a Midwestern suburb. I read the Bible in a completely different way than that of a

Latin American woman struggling in destitute poverty under the oppressive rule of a dictatorship. The subjective experience of our lives magnifies certain aspects of Scripture while reducing the importance of others.

Such unavoidable subjectivity is anything but a descent into meaningless relativism. The fact that our subjective experience colors the way we read Scripture isn't a surprise to God. That's part of the beauty and mystery of Scripture. The stories of the Bible are remarkably adept at speaking to people in wildly divergent contexts. We must remember that the Bible is not merely—or even primarily—a collection of objective propositions. It is a grand story told through hundreds of different perspectives and diverse social settings. The message is multilayered, textured, expansive, and complex.

The mere fact that the Bible includes four versions of the life of Jesus shows us that the subjective experience of each author offers something unique and important to our faith. This subjectivity helps paint a more colorful picture. By acknowledging and owning the limits of our own subjectivity, our soul remains open and limber, available for growth, development, and discovery.

But when objectivity is taken to the extreme, it erodes both our humanity and our humility.

Into Thin Air

Eighteenth-century revivalist Jonathan Edwards often preached sermons that lasted four hours.[2] George

Whitefield, a contemporary of Edwards, preached a sermon entitled "A Preservative against unsettled Notions, and want of Principles, in regard to Righteousness and Christian Perfection."[3] Try putting that on the church billboard—it sounds more like a doctoral dissertation than a sermon. Move beyond the title, and you will discover that it is written with the same complex reasoning, lengthy sentence construction, and dense technical language characteristic of a contemporary academic paper.

You might presume these sermons were written for an academic audience. On the contrary, these were the great revival sermons of the day. Edwards and Whitefield were to the eighteenth century what Billy Graham was to the twentieth century. Their sermons were so influential they became the primary force behind the Great Awakening, which gave birth to the modern evangelical movement in America.[4]

While these preachers had great intellects, their influence reveals more about the nature of their audiences. I don't know many people today who could sit through a four-hour sermon, let alone be moved to tears and convert on the spot. But in a culture so thoroughly shaped by the printed word, those eighteenth-century audiences not only had the capacity to receive these sermons, but given the stunning response, they seemed to prefer this style.

Printing makes us think in more abstract terms. In a culture without writing, once knowledge is acquired, it has to be continually repeated or it will be lost. As a result, thought patterns demand streamlining and simplification. They also focus thinking on things that can be seen and touched.

Oral tradition is marked by stories about sheep, burning bushes, healings, and talking donkeys. They don't spend much time on invisible things like "perfection," "sanctification," "justice," or "truth." But the spread of the printed word allows knowledge to climb further into the thin air of abstraction and elaboration without the threat of losing any of the previous thoughts. Before you know it, sermons are being preached entitled "A Preservative against unsettled Notions, and want of Principles, in regard to Righteousness and Christian Perfection."

Of course, all of this may seem (*you're an individual*) like quite a reach. Who knows if what (*remain objective*) I'm saying is even (*think abstractly*) true?

CHAPTER 6

ElectricFaith

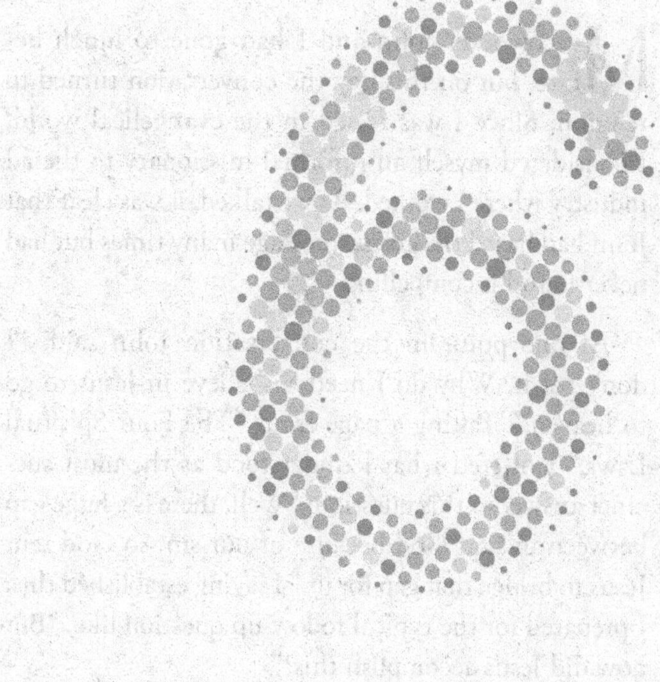

My coworker John and I had gone to lunch before, but on this day the conversation turned to religion. Since I was raised in the evangelical world, I considered myself an informal missionary to the ad industry where I worked. As we talked, it was clear that John had heard the gospel message many times but had never found it compelling.

At one point in the conversation John said, "I don't get it. Why do I need to believe in Jesus to go to heaven?" Taking a page from "The Four Spiritual Laws," I offered what I understood as the most succinct answer to this question: "Well, there is a huge gap between us and God because of our sin, so God sent Jesus to bridge that gap for us." Having established this, I prepared for the typical follow-up question like, "But how did Jesus accomplish this?"

The question never came.

Instead, John responded by saying, "I don't think there *is* any gap between me and God, so I guess I don't need Jesus."

I wasn't prepared for that, but I pressed on. I informed John that the Bible tells us there *is* a gap between us and God. He cordially responded, "I realize that, but the Bible is *your* authority. Don't get me wrong; I think that's cool. It's just not *my* authority." Over the course of the conversation I emptied my arsenal of apologetic munitions on him — C. S. Lewis, Josh McDowell, Bill Hybels. He was polite, but none of it stuck. It was like trying to nail Jell-O to the wall.

This conversation initiated a crisis of faith for me. I began to realize that I had all the answers to the questions no one was asking. I went on a search that led me quite unexpectedly out of advertising and my evangelical upbringing to seminary and the Mennonite tradition of faith.

During my search I made an important discovery. John's strange way of thinking wasn't unique to him. He was a product of a fundamental shift in culture — a culture increasingly governed by the beliefs of so-called "moral relativism," which asserts that there is no absolute truth with a capital *T*. There is only my truth and your truth. Both are fine, even if they contradict.

The Victorian Internet

John doesn't know this, but his way of looking at the world began in 1832 on a voyage across the Atlantic Ocean. Aboard the ship was a struggling artist named Samuel F. B. Morse, traveling from England to America. It was then that he first became enamored by the possibility of communicating using electricity. Twelve years later, on May 24, 1844, Morse established the first electric communication, which was sent between Baltimore and Washington, D. C. His now famous—and prophetic—inaugural message exclaimed simply, "What hath God wrought?"[1]

That same year the German philosopher Friedrich Nietzsche was born. By 1883, forty years after the first telegraph message was sent, Nietzsche declared the death of God. His proclamation is widely acknowledged as a harbinger of the end of the modern age. One of the hallmarks of modernity was the belief in the existence of absolute Truth. Nietzsche is considered the father of the age that followed—known as postmodernity. And John's reasoning is a perfect reflection of the sensibilities of this age.

In a very real way, the telegraph helped plant the seeds of the postmodern age. As McLuhan once observed, "We shape our tools and afterward our tools shape us."[2]

Morse's invention dramatically altered the way we relate to information by breaking, for the first time, the historic connection between communication and transportation. Prior to the telegraph, information traveled at about 35 miles per hour—roughly the speed of a train.[3] But when information was translated into an electric pulse, it was freed to travel at the speed of light. This spectacular technological breakthrough would alter more than just the way people communicated—it would change their worldview.

Throughout the millennia that preceded the telegraph, information was local, rooted in a context, and wrapped in history to provide meaning and coherence. Most printed material came in the form of books, which provided lengthy context and interpretive meaning. With the telegraph, information was torn from its local and historical setting. It was presented in newspaper form as a mosaic of unrelated headlines with no obvious connection to one another.

Prior to the telegraph, information was mostly presented in books and organized for the purpose of deepening our understanding and wisdom. But with the telegraph, information increasingly became a commodity in itself, something that could be bought and sold. Its price was determined by how fast and how far it traveled, not whether it was meaningful or useful.

As Neil Postman observes, "The principal strength of the telegraph was its capacity to move information, not collect it, explain it, or analyze it."[4] As a result, information itself changed to the point where "there is no sense of proportion to be discerned in the world. Events are entirely idiosyncratic; history is irrelevant; there is no rational basis for valuing one thing over another."[5]

It is easy to be awed by the wide-reaching power of the Internet, yet it is the logical extension—an unimaginably vast extension, to be sure—of the telegraph. Today we are swallowed by a swarm of unrelated facts accorded equal importance—"Two Marines Killed in Iraq" ... "Britney Spears in Car Accident" ... "Bin Laden Issues New Video." Our challenge becomes figuring out how to prioritize and find meaning in this mosaic of events. Most of them simply fill our brain with useless trivia. This glut of disparate, often contradictory, and random data with no center or periphery becomes the window through which we see the world.

As the telegraph wrapped the world in a web of wires, it began to whisper a new subliminal message: *Truth* itself must be a lot like information. The idea of "Truth" becomes "entirely idiosyncratic; history is irrelevant; there is no rational basis for valuing one thing over another." Because our thinking mirrors the pattern of our media, eventually we find it only natural to deny the existence of absolute Truth, an overarching story that organizes and makes sense of all other truths.

As a result, authority, truth, and meaning become difficult to discover and establish with clarity or certainty. Doubts trickle in, and we find the notion of a single grand story that unifies everything to be absurd and even arrogant. In this sense, the telegraph tapped out the obituary of absolute Truth and created the conditions necessary to usher in the postmodern age.

Puberty of the Mind

To a hammer, all the world is a nail. To a math wizard, all the world is a problem to be solved. Sergey Brin and Larry Page are the math wizards who founded Google. They are hoping to solve the world's problems one algorithm at a time. The company's mission is "to organize the world's information and make it universally accessible and useful." They want to make us more productive and efficient thinkers who can sift through the world's information more quickly.[6]

The last word in that mission statement is *useful.* Information can certainly be useful. Knowing how to build a well in a country with no infrastructure and little rainfall comes in very handy. The knowledge that washing your hands can prevent disease is also quite useful.

However, what happens when we have access to too much information? The sheer volume of information accessible to the world has been increasing at breakneck pace, and shows no signs of slowing. Consider the number of volumes required to produce the first Encyclopedia Britannica. The first edition, published in 1771, required only one editor, three volumes, and about 2,500 pages to encapsulate nearly everything thought to be worth knowing. For a hundred years, knowledge expanded at a modest pace, and by 1860 the Encyclopedia required a few hundred contributors spanning twenty-one volumes and about 18,000 pages. This was the time when speed-of-light communication began to transform the information game—and transform the acquisition of knowledge as well. By 1970, the number of contributors to the Encyclopedia had soared to over 10,000, and the 30 volumes contained increasingly brief articles. Today, the Encyclopedia Britannica is almost totally irrelevant, having been replaced by online resources like Wikipedia, which features an endless and perpetual expansion of articles now reaching well into the millions. In this space there is no single editor who determines what stays and what goes, only the "wisdom" and morality of the anonymous digital mob.

Some have suggested that this quintessentially democratic editorial process is more trustworthy than a conventional encyclopedia because anyone can make a correction. However, recently developed software called Wiki Scanner is able to track anonymous edits on Wikipedia. It reveals something unsettling but perhaps not surprising. The largest number of edits were made by major corporations like Diebold Election Systems, Exxon, or government agencies like the CIA. They were all surreptitiously deleting or changing any references they could find that were unflattering to them or contradicted the company line.[7]

The problem is not only misinformation. Even when accurate, information glut causes problems of its own. Thamus's critique of writing in Plato's *Phaedrus* is perhaps more applicable to information systems like the Internet. He tells the inventor of writing that people "will receive a quantity of information without proper instruction, and in consequence be thought very knowledgeable when they are for the most part quite ignorant. And because they are filled with the conceit of wisdom instead of real wisdom they will be a burden to society."[8]

Thamus correctly points out that there are important differences between information, understanding, and wisdom.

The journey of adolescence illustrates this. Back in my high school days, Travis hit puberty way before the rest of us. While we were still ninety-eight pound weaklings, he was big, fast, and muscle-bound. Unfortunately, he lacked the ability to coordinate those muscles meaningfully. As a result, in those early days he was often more of a danger to himself than others.

In time, Travis developed coordination that matched his strength. By then he dominated in sports—especially as the middle linebacker on our football team. Now he was no longer a danger to himself—he was a danger to others. Lining up opposite him was only a good idea if you liked the experience of blackouts and agony. Eventually, as Travis got comfortable in his own power, he became a person who used his strength in restrained and protective ways.

Information alone is strength without coordination. We become a danger mostly to ourselves when we have it. Understanding is the ability to coordinate that raw information in meaningful ways. Understanding creates a certain enthusiasm. We can direct our knowledge toward potentially useful ends—but we may also be a danger to others. Wisdom, however, is knowing how, when, and why we use our understanding; wisdom is settling into our understanding without being too enamored by it.

The Internet encourages only the knowledge-gathering stage without considering coordination or meaningful connections. Despite Google and Wikipedia's best efforts, understanding is not born of the answers algorithms provide—answers and understanding are not the same thing. Some will sift through the answers and information, seek to coordinate it, and emerge with understanding—but this is still not the same as wisdom.

Unfortunately, the Information Age does little to encourage the development of wisdom. This requires time, experience, contemplation, patience, suffering, and even stillness to obtain. But the churning sea of information never settles long enough to allow for the emergence of wisdom. We are left instead with "the conceit of wisdom rather than real wisdom" and become a burden to society rather than a boon.

If we are not alert, the Information Age may stunt our growth and create a permanent puberty of the mind.

CHAPTER 7

A Thousand Feelings

I am on a plane, scanning a once-gray tray table in front of me. It is now fully covered by a decal of an ad. The image depicts an uninspiring and unrecognizable city skyline. A headline reads "Sparkling, shimmering, scintillating Montreal." The copy of the ad beckons me to visit, and while I've never been to Montreal and have nothing against it, I remain unmoved. They're going to have to do better than a listless ad to get me to change my travel habits. After all, in the time it took me to get from my house to the airport, I've already been assaulted by thousands of messages trying to persuade me to do something or buy something I wasn't planning to do or buy that day. Advertising is the ever-present I AM of our global economy, and next time you feel like cursing its crass and intrusive ubiquity, you can direct your angst toward a single invention —the camera.

In the mid-nineteenth century, the photographic camera was invented which, when joined in unholy matrimony with the rotary press and the telegraph, gave birth to the Graphic Revolution. Advertisers quickly realized that images have an incredible capacity to generate needs in humans that don't naturally exist. Every part of our lives is influenced and shaped by the power of the photograph.

The Worth of a Picture

If a picture is worth a thousand words, then images must communicate information more efficiently than words. The truism contains another assumption, however—that one medium can function interchangeably with the other. While there may not be a one-to-one correspondence, images and words seem to be competing for the same job. In reality, however, neither medium can accomplish what the other can. I could not convey the ideas contained in this book using only images—the form blocks the content. Neither could I do it with interpretive dance, although it might generate the next big YouTube sensation.

The truth is that words and images are fundamentally different modes of communication that have totally different effects. Consider the content below.

The boy is sad.

What effect does this have on you? For most of us, it is a statement that conveys an idea devoid of any real emotional significance. Now turn the page to consider the same content in a different medium.

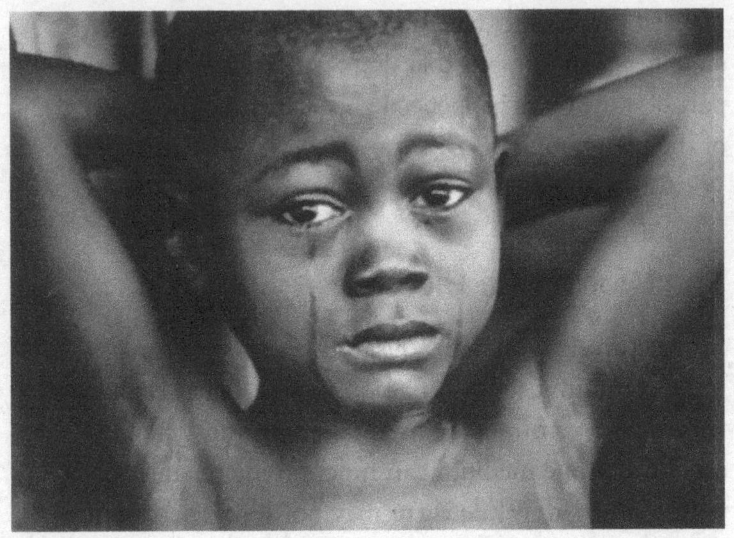

Does this image affect you differently? It probably makes you feel sad. While the basic *content* of the image is the same as that conveyed in the printed description, the *impact* is, for most of us, radically different. So it would seem a picture is actually worth a thousand feelings.

Images initially make us *feel* rather than *think*. They can pin the logical side of your brain to the back of your skull, which is why image-based advertising is so effective. Images don't invite you to argue; they give you an experience. In contrast, the printed word makes us think and question. The statement "The boy is sad" generates several logical questions: Which boy? How sad? Why? But one look at the image leaves no doubt of the boy's sadness.

Our brains process printed words and images in different ways. The printed word is processed primarily in the left hemisphere of the brain, which specializes in logic, sequence, and categories. Images are processed primarily in the right hemisphere, which specializes in intuition and holistic perception rather than linear analysis. I apprehend an image all at once, while I read text word-by-word and line-by-line.

Image culture dramatically shapes the way we think. It also determines what we think about. Images are not well-suited to articulate arguments, categories, or abstractions. They are far better suited for presenting impressions and experiences.

One consequence is that our political discourse is now based on intuition rather than reason. A presidential candidate is more likely to be elected if he appears capable, attractive, and trustworthy. These are subjective and intuitive evaluations based almost entirely on visual images. The left-brained analysis of a candidate's policy positions becomes secondary and thoroughly uninteresting. In the most basic sense, the image reduces our capacity for abstract thought and heightens our appreciation of intuition and emotion.

Brain Candy

Most parents I know are masters in the art of redirection. If you can distract a kid just before he leaps from the sofa onto the cat, you just might extend the peace and quiet for a few more minutes—and if the redirection is absorbing enough, you just might get something accomplished. Most parents try not to use the nuclear option more often than they have to, but desperate times call for desperate measures—and on comes the television. But television is a double-edged sword. Many parents experience a vague feeling of guilt when plopping junior in front of the tube, so marketers have worked to assuage that guilt by providing things like Baby Einstein videos or TiVo. Never mind that the American Academy of Pediatrics warns that children should not watch television before the age of two, or that studies have linked early viewing with an increased risk of Attention Deficit Disorder, autism, aggression, obesity, and possibly dyslexia.[1]

While these studies may be on to something, my concern has more to do with the subtle and invisible consequences of television. These consequences have nothing to do with the programming—whether you've got a Baby Einstein video playing or the latest abomination in reality TV, it's the *medium*, not the *content*, that changes us. Believe it or not, the flickering mosaic of pixilated light repatterns neural pathways in the brain. These new pathways are simply opposed to the pathways required for reading, writing, and sustained concentration.

The television image is extraordinarily stimulating to the brain, and not in a healthy, "this discussion about politics is so *stimulating*" way—more like the sugar-is-stimulating-to-the-body way. The televised brain candy we consume doesn't develop—or even require—any mental capacity.

Reading, on the other hand, is brain protein—it demands concentration and sustained neural energy. This practice is also generative. Powerful capacities are created which are not naturally developed by the brain, resulting in ever-more nuanced skills of discernment, logic, and reasoning. The underrated virtue of patience is also developed by reading, since it requires one to be seated, focused, and disciplined for extended periods of time. While television also invites long periods of focused time, it encourages a catatonic state rather than an engaged one.

The good news is that children are resilient little creatures; regardless of their youthful media habits, they'll survive. But we have a chance to make their life easier in a culture that demands the mastery of reading and writing. All it takes is the push of a button. Who knew it could be this simple?

Just to be clear, I didn't promise it would be easy.

Hijacking Imagination

I love movies, but there is one thing that bugs me and everyone else I know: A movie based on a book is *never* as good as the book. For this we can thank the fundamental difference in how words and images affect us.

In the simplest sense, written words stimulate and liberate the imagination. Images, on the other hand, usually captivate the imagination. When you read the statement "The boy is sad," your mind could create any image it desired for that statement. The number of possibilities was only limited by the amount of time spent thinking about them. But when you saw the picture of the sad boy, the image fed you every last detail. There was only one specific possibility, so your imagination was no longer required. These differences make it impossible for the finite choices of a movie director to match the infinite choices of a book's readers.

The mind was made to generate, create, and imagine. Creative imagination is a fundamental stage of brain development that begins very early in life. Kids naturally learn how to pretend. So when the mind generates a vast array of imagined pictures to bring a story to life, and then has them summarily replaced by the images of a movie, it is deeply unsatisfying.

In a very real way, image culture is eroding and undermining imaginative creativity. Imagination is extremely important to our functioning as healthy, creative people. This goes way beyond the creation of good art or entertainment—our imaginations are what help us change the world.

A weakened imagination means it will be increasingly hard for us to solve the problems that confront us on a daily basis. Our minds become lethargic and passive beneath the torrent of images, simply awaiting fresh stimulation. From important personal decisions to difficult relationships, and from local politics to global concerns, we simply won't be equipped—or even able—to engage in creative and effective solutions or connections.

This malaise even affects what we might call spiritual imagination. This is the kind of daring imagination that helps us expand our experience and understanding of God, the kind of imagination that allows us to enact God's compassion in a broken world. In a world this complex and dangerous, a vivid spiritual imagination is crucial for helping us enact the call to love our enemy and bring about reconciliation in places of deep brokenness.

The Resuscitation of Jesus

Images give and take away. I have focused mostly on the taking away. But not all is lost. There was one unexpected gift of image culture. The photograph led to the resuscitation of the person of Jesus as central to our faith. You may be surprised to learn that Jesus went out of fashion during the print age.

In his translation of the New Testament, Martin Luther offered an evaluation of the New Testament. In a section entitled "Which Are the True and Noblest Books of the New Testament?" Luther writes, "John's gospel is the one, fine, true, and chief gospel, and is far, far to be preferred over the other three and placed high above them. So, too, the epistles of St. Paul and St. Peter far surpass the other three gospels, Matthew, Mark, and Luke."[2]

Luther's reasoning was simple—anything in Scripture that tells the *story of* Jesus was of little value as compared to those writings that describe explicit *doctrines about* Jesus. It should not surprise us that Luther, who was shaped by the printed word, would elevate these books. John's gospel and the letters of Peter and Paul are made up of highly theological monologues or long conversations. Matthew, Mark, and Luke, on the other hand, are characterized by short stories and parables rooted in the thought patterns of an oral tradition.

Luther observed that John, Peter, and Paul provide us with a theology of Christ while Matthew, Mark, and Luke *merely* provide us with the life of Jesus.

In an image-saturated culture, the concrete life-stories of Jesus gain traction once again. The age of image restores a right-brain preference for parable and story over theology and doctrine. The life of Jesus is just that—a story. As a consequence, the life of Jesus is slowly becoming the interpretive center of the New Testament.

Much of evangelical Christianity is witnessing a subtle shift from its heritage of abstract doctrine to the concrete ethics. That means we are more focused today on how we behave rather than how we believe. Bracelets remind us to consider "What Would Jesus Do?" not "What Would Jesus Believe?" This approach to Christianity finds expression increasingly through the language of "following" rather than "believing." Many are learning to prefer the designation of "Christ-follower" rather than "Christian."

The shift from emphasizing our intellectual *beliefs* to the ethics of *following* is a direct consequence of the influence of images. A belief is located firmly in the realm of the invisible and abstract. A belief is something that happens in the mind. But *following* is located in the world of the visible and concrete. Following is what happens in daily life.

In reality, beliefs and behaviors are inseparable. However, depending on the dominant medium of a culture, one is emphasized over the other. During the print age, concrete practice went out of fashion in favor of abstract beliefs. The print age gave birth to an academic discipline known as Systematic Theology. The point of this discipline is to scan the Scriptures in order to extract, organize, and codify abstract propositional truths and doctrines. It forms the core curriculum for most seminary educations. One renowned Systematic Theology professor at my seminary told his students not to attempt to use this discipline for any practical purpose; it is intended exclusively for academic concerns. A startling injunction for young seminarians filled with dreams of ministering to people in the mud of life.

Under the force of image culture and our growing interest in practice, a new academic discipline is emerging known as Practical Theology. This discipline is convinced that practice should inform theology, and theology should inform practice. It sees them as inseparable.

The shift toward behavior over belief is not merely an academic one. It actually forms an answer to the most pressing question of my friend John. In the course of our conversation, I learned something. I learned that I had all the answers to the questions he wasn't asking. I knew (or thought I knew) how to get him in to heaven. But that isn't what interested him. He didn't believe in heaven or hell. He didn't care what my beliefs did for me in the next life. He wanted to know what my faith did for others while I was here. This is a question of ethics. How does your faith actually manifest in this world to bring about justice, altruism, compassion, and peace? He didn't say it that way, but that is what he was asking. And so this shift to ethics resonates with people like John. In this approach, belief is not absent or irrelevant. Instead, our beliefs are judged by their fruit—how they change the world while we're here.

Depending upon your perspective, this shift is either a liberating confirmation of what you already thought, or it is a disconcerting threat to the faith. In either case, you have images to blame or thank. The point is that our theology and practice are deeply informed and shaped by our media and technology. We become what we behold.

CHAPTER 8

The Dimmer Switch

T[illegible] of Jesus. Here's a guy who [illegible] up every[illegible] and followed Jesus for three [illegible]. When Jesus d[illegible]mas went into hiding with the other disciples. [illegible]er appeared before the dis[illegible] Thomas [illegible] buying it. He didn't believe th[illegible]. So he decided to kick the tires [illegible] his han[illegible]ly in the open wounds of Jes[illegible] not sure I would have been so bold. Apparently [illegible] didn't mind, and it's a good thing, because in that moment Thomas became a believer.

[illegible] I wonder what would have happened if Thomas [illegible] before his finger touched the wounds. [illegible] followed Jesus faithfully for three years as a friend and a disciple, but in that last moment before touching Jesus' wounds he didn't really believe. Thomas was a follower of Jesus who wasn't a believer. What do we do with this category of person? What does that mean for his eternal destiny?

This question could be extended to the other disciples as well. When was each converted? When was

Thomas was a disciple of Jesus. Here's a guy who gave up everything and followed Jesus for three years. When Jesus died, Thomas went into hiding with the other disciples. Jesus later appeared before the disciples, but Thomas wasn't buying it. He didn't believe that this ghost was his Rabbi. So he decided to kick the tires. He poked his finger directly in the open wounds of Jesus. I'm not sure I would have been so bold. Apparently, Jesus didn't mind, and it's a good thing, because in that moment Thomas became a believer.

Sometimes I wonder what would have happened if Thomas had died just seconds before his finger touched the wound. This man followed Jesus faithfully for three years as a friend and a disciple, but in that last moment before touching Jesus' wounds he didn't truly believe. Thomas was a follower of Jesus who wasn't a believer. What do we do with this category of person? What does that mean for his eternal destiny?

This question could be extended to the other disciples as well. When was each converted? When was

Peter saved? Asking such questions begins to reveal the hazards of our modern obsession with determining exact moments of—and definitions for—conversion. In the text, the gospel writers don't seem as concerned as we can be. Conversion for the disciples was marked by an unfolding series of discoveries. Their conversion was not a single event so much as a gradual process.

More of a dimmer switch than a light switch.

This is in stark contrast to Paul's story. Paul had the dramatic, binary light switch moment on his way to Damascus. One day he's issuing murderous threats against the disciples, and the next day he's one of them. One day he's the persecutor, the next he's the persecuted. The Bible presents us with at least two different understandings of conversion, and yet, depending on the cultural context, one understanding is always emphasized at the expense of the other.

The Light Switch

In college I attended a weekly Bible study at a local evangelical church. For eight weeks we watched a video series about evangelism. We learned how to strategically build relationships with "non-believers," as well as the most effective strategies to help those people move from the "unsaved" column in God's accounting ledger to the "saved" column.

I'll tell you how it works so you don't have to sit through all eight videos. Once I built a trusting relationship with a non-believer, my job was to help them see that their beliefs were mostly wrong. Like a mechanic, I was trained to lift the hood of their head and tinker around with their brain until they had all the right beliefs organized in the right way. Any erroneous beliefs could be tossed out along with any impure thoughts. Once the beliefs were properly organized, and the person spoke those beliefs aloud so I could hear them, a switch was flipped in heaven: From then on, the former non-believer was a heaven-bound Christian.

This on/off understanding of conversion finds roots in the Bible. Paul writes in Romans, "If you confess with your mouth, 'Jesus is Lord,' and believe in your heart that God raised him from the dead, you will be saved."[1] The implication is that this happens in an instant. One minute you're doomed, and the next you're saved.

This metaphor became the guiding example of conversion during the print age and the evangelical faith that grew from it. This is partly a consequence of the medium of print. The printed word creates fissures in the mind. It makes us prefer distinctions between things. Printing breeds a strong preference for categories.

This is true of language in general, but the medium of print turbo-charges this capacity. The print-saturated mind is enamored with classification, categories, and elaboration. Such ability can be extremely useful. It helps bring order from chaos. This is one reason God told Adam to name the animals in the garden. God wanted Adam to bring order and meaning to a chaotic world. However, when overused or applied to the wrong things, we can run into problems. This fetish for categories can be most troubling when applied to people and faith.

Many of the categories we create don't exist in reality. They are invented through language. The categories of "apples" and "oranges" don't exist until we create them with our words. We invent and overlay these labels on reality to organize and tidy up our world. This can be extremely useful in the case of the sciences, where these categories can be verified through direct and empirical observation. They can then be further divided and sub-divided into other categories — "McIntosh," "Golden Delicious," "Fuji." Then there are internal categories — "stem," "core," "seeds," "skin."

But in the case of categories of consciousness or states of mind, things are more fluid. The categorical shift from "non-believer" to "believer," or "unsaved" to "saved" are rarely stable, clear, and binary equations or events. These conditions are more like waves. Determining the strict boundary of a wave is like trying to determine exactly when the dawn becomes the day. Or when confidence becomes arrogance. Or when admiration becomes envy. These things exist on an analog continuum. Nonetheless, during the age of print these categories of consciousness and eternal destiny were codified and entrenched.

However, as images displace the word, our thinking patterns and preferences change. Increasingly, the metaphor of Thomas and the dimmer switch is our preferred way of imagining the life of faith. A photograph doesn't separate and make distinctions (left-brain);

rather it depicts wholes and continuums (right-brain). Images depict the unity of reality rather than discrete binary ideas. They do not explain or organize the world the way language can.

In time we learn to show appreciation and even preference for all things holistic (right-brain). We learn to love life's unified continuums—the very things images can best depict.[2] As images dominate our world, our preoccupation with creating discrete categories becomes less interesting or urgent. Our culture comes to believe that strict categories oversimplify the complex mystery of God's relationship to God's people and the dynamic reality of a life of faith. Categorization is still alive and well in our culture, but the emphasis and importance is waning.

I remember reading books like *Evidence That Demands a Verdict* by Josh McDowell, a classic evangelism tool for the print era. McDowell's method is rooted in the debates of a courtroom, which stress clearly opposing categories of good and evil, right and wrong, saved and unsaved.

In contrast, people saturated in image culture are beginning to prefer metaphors like gardening, dialogue, or dancing for describing evangelism. These metaphors emphasize the process, the continual ebb and flow of two or more people seeking truth together in an ongoing state of humble discovery. The moment when a person is moved from the "unsaved" category to the "saved" category is less important than the unfolding process of growth. In an image culture, static categories for evangelism, discipleship, and salvation are increasingly difficult to define and maintain—pronouncement is replaced by process.

All around us, images are tearing down walls and serving as a helpful corrective to the tyranny of fixed categories. Now, many are coming to believe that robust faith lives somewhere between absolute trust and deep doubt. The colors of faith change through seasons of grief and hope, passion and despair. No one has it all figured out all the time—both Christians and non-Christians are in need of ongoing conversion. Humanity as a whole is called to participate in an unfolding process of redemption and reconciliation.

A good friend of mine goes to church every week and is convinced that he's supposed to act like Jesus. He is one of the most authentic followers of Jesus I know. But he also wrestles with doubts—serious doubts. He has a very hard time accepting that Jesus was divine or could have possibly been raised from the dead. He just can't seem to get there.

According to static categories of the print gospel, my friend is headed for hell until he gets his beliefs straight in his mind. He needs a good dose of Pauline theology if he wants to score high enough on his doctrine test to get a saving score. But my friend has far more in common with Thomas than with Paul—more in common with the anguished father who tells Jesus, "I do believe; help me overcome my unbelief!"[3]

Image culture is learning to make space for this kind of person. The person who is a true follower of Jesus, a student and a learner, but perhaps not yet—and maybe not ever—an orthodox believer. This category of doubting disciple didn't seem to bother Jesus; after all, his parting words to us in the book of Matthew were, "Therefore go and make disciples ..."[4] Jesus didn't tell us to make *believers*. He called us to make *disciples*, and disciples are followers and students of the way of God. Followers learn to change their beliefs as they walk.

Conversion can feel like a light switch has been flipped from off to on, and everything is suddenly illuminated. Conversion can also feel like the gradual brightening of a long darkness—or like a long fade from clarity into doubt. Jesus, it would seem, joins us in both the darkness and the light. In both sudden epiphany and unhurried evolution.

CHAPTER 9

SoulStealing

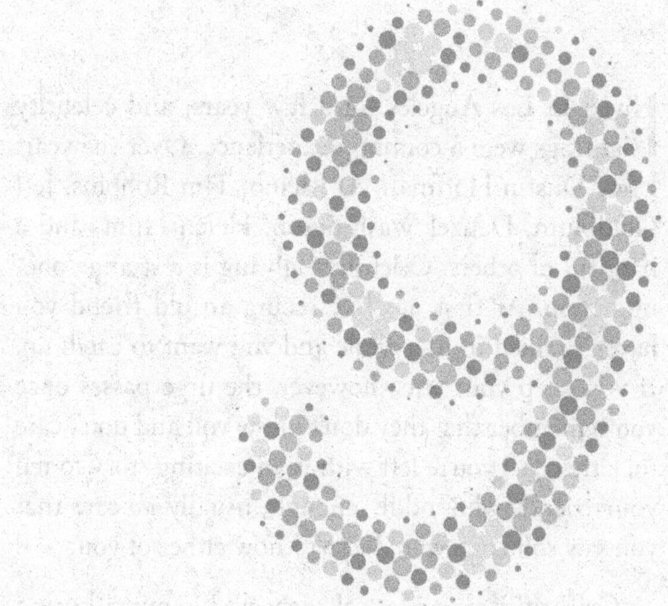

I lived in Los Angeles for a few years, and celebrity sightings were a common experience. Over the years I saw Dustin Hoffman, Al Pacino, Tim Robbins, Jeff Goldblum, Denzel Washington, Helen Hunt, and a handful of others. Celebrity sighting is a strange phenomenon. At first, it's like seeing an old friend you haven't talked to in a while and you want to catch up. If you keep your wits, however, the urge passes once you remember that they don't know you and don't care to, either. All you're left with is an exciting story to tell your friends who, oddly enough, usually *do* care that you saw someone who doesn't know either of you.

Celebrities are a relatively new class in our culture, a class that didn't exist prior to the invention of the photograph. Former generations had "heroes," people who were well-known for remarkable feats of bravery, brilliance, creativity, or self-sacrifice. Heroes earned their status. Celebrities, on the other hand, are well-known mostly for being well-known.[1] We all know exactly who Paris Hilton and Fabio are, but we'd be hard-pressed to name a single accomplishment. We have the image to thank for this.

Most nineteenth-century Americans viewed photographs as an exciting kind of magic, but some cultures are deeply suspicious of the camera. Certain African tribes believe the camera possesses mysterious powers that can steal your soul. The Amish reject the photographic image for fear that it will develop in people excessive vanity and pride. Neither group is entirely wrong.

Consider someone like Britney Spears: Photographs — and our voyeuristic enjoyment of them — have disabused her of her soul, that place of grounded centering. She was made into an object rather than a person. She may have started believing her own image and lost her sense of self. This is not uncommon, especially among young celebrities. Without a center, her life started spinning out of control with disastrous consequences. It's not that she's a victim — she craved fame and worked hard to attain it — but the image gives and the image takes away. She can never again be related to as a real person, but only as a persona. Consider the fate of Princess Diana as an extreme example of the photograph's ability to steal a soul. Her death was a direct result of our insatiable appetite for images. To condemn the paparazzi is like condemning the butcher while eating a steak.

So it turns out that the Africans and the Amish were right — sort of.

The Amish fear of vanity *has* played out, though often in an unexpected way. The photograph contributes to the growing narcissism in our culture. Unlike Narcissus, however, whose self-obsession was excessive self-love, our self-obsession often takes the form of excessive self-loathing.

A friend of mine has a lean, active, and beautiful eight-year-old daughter who asked one day, "Mom, do I look fat?" The question was jarring and absurd, and the answer was an emphatic "No!" But the question indicates that the natural self-consciousness of adolescence is now beginning much earlier. Equally disconcerting is that this body-image crisis of our culture now dogs us decades after adolescence has subsided. What are we to make of this addict-like preoccupation with our looks? First, you should know this: It's not your fault. Really. It's not your fault.

Pixel Perfect

A few years ago Dove launched an ad campaign called "Real Beauty." It boldly sought to expose and correct the body-image problem in our culture—and, of course, sell basketfuls of Dove products. The campaign aimed to change our culture's narrow definition of beauty beyond the artificial perfection of models and movie stars.

One ad featured a split-screen shot of a model's face. It was a "before" and "after" shot. That is, "before" makeup, hair, and the all-important post-production retouching, and then "after." The extent of the retouching on the "after" shot was astonishing. The model didn't merely receive smoother cheeks and flawless skin tone. The size of her eyes was increased, her neck was lengthened, her lips plumped up, and her jaw line was completely reshaped. It was no longer the same woman, or even a real woman at all. She had become pixilated perfection.

How noble of Dove to expose the dirty tricks that advertisers use to make us feel unsatisfied with our bodies. Yet their campaign had its own little secret. The man responsible for the image retouching of the Dove ads is a legendary digital artist named Pascal Dangin. Insiders describe him as the "photo whisperer"—able to coax unimagined beauty from nearly any image. In an interview with *The New Yorker*, Dangin was asked about the Dove campaign. Referring to the "before" images he said, "Do you know how much retouching was on that? But it was great to do, a challenge, to keep everyone's skin and faces showing the mileage but not looking unattractive."[2]

That's right, the natural "before" image is as artificial as the "after" image.

Our culture has descended to a place where even the natural beauty of a supermodel is simply not beautiful enough to withstand the unflinching scrutiny of the camera. The most "beautiful" individuals in the world must be thoroughly transformed before being shown to the public. Is it any wonder that eight-year-old girls are already questioning their own self-image? The medium of images draws our attention away from the inner life and toward the appearance of things, and this has serious implications for the soul.

Ripped Abs and Wrinkles

I visited a church that was launching several new worship gatherings in different locations around the city. I watched the preacher in person while, miles from me, three other campuses watched the sermon on large video screens. This is part of a growing trend. Churches pastored by highly talented communicators may desire to extend the reach of the message, but may still want to retain the personal feel of a smaller service. These "video venue" services try to combine the astonishing reach of a televised event with the community experience of the local church.

This preacher was certainly gifted. He was handsome, poised, funny, and conversational. In his sermon, he illustrated the difference between talent and character. On stage next to him sat a huge dictionary, and as he spoke, he began to dispense several cans of whipped cream on top of the dictionary, creating a white, fluffy mound. When he finished, he told us that the dictionary was our character, the firm foundation. The whipped cream was our talent, something attractive but lacking ultimate substance. "If your life is based on character," he said, "it will last, but if your life is based on talent ..."—he swiped the mound of whipped cream onto the floor—"you will suffer when times get tough."

The message he wanted to convey is that character matters more than talent, and the deep things in life matter more than the surface. But he was saying this through a televised event. This is important because the medium of video actually magnifies talent, not character. It inadvertently creates celebrity. In this case, the medium undermined his message. This doesn't mean that anyone whose image is projected on a video medium is devoid of character. Rather, it just means that projecting one's image on film neither encourages nor requires depth of character. A televangelist can have millions of viewers and as many moral failings. Television, film, and video are powerful generators of emotional experience. This is their great strength. When used in the hands of a skillful artist, they can open and penetrate deeper realities. But most of the time images direct us to the surface of things.

Images focus our attention on the realm of cosmetics. Often, it is for the sake of showcasing beauty and talent. It teaches us to scrutinize not just others, but also ourselves. Thinning hair, splotchy skin, love handles, cellulite, stretch marks, and wrinkles become sources of preoccupation, depression, and great effort.

The funny thing is, Jesus never talked much about thick hair, ripped abs, youthful skin, or sexy legs. Paul never mentioned any of these when he listed the fruit of the Spirit, and yet our energetic pursuit of everything on the surface seems to say otherwise.

Think back to the last time you looked at a photograph of yourself in a group of people. What was the first thing you looked at? It wasn't the other people. It was you. And then the scrutiny begins:

"Whoa, I look pretty pasty."

"I'm never wearing *that* shirt again."

"Oh, how's the double chin treating me?"

Not to worry—your true friends will offer reassuring consolations like, "Oh, you don't look like that at all, that's just a bad angle." So we simultaneously blame *that* image for making us look bad and *trust* that the next image will make us look better and restore some of our self-worth.

Maybe God was on to something when he commanded his people not to make graven images.

CHAPTER 10

TogetherApart

A few years ago, AT&T launched an ad campaign for its mobile phone services. In it, a business traveler checks into a stark and lifeless motel room. He sits alone on the bed, dejected and lonely. The ad then cuts to him sitting in an airport after his flight has been delayed. A close-up of the man's face reveals despair and resignation. Alone. Again.

From out of nowhere, we then hear the sweet voice of a little girl. "Hi, Daddy," she says. We cut to a wide shot to reveal his five-year-old daughter now magically seated next to him. The man beams, and he begins laughing and talking with his daughter.

As they talk, the bustle of pedestrians obscures our view of the little girl and her dad. The moment the pedestrians pass, the scene changes. The seat where his daughter was is now empty. The business traveler is alone again, only he is still happy. It turns out that he's talking on his cell phone with his little girl, exuding the same elation as when his daughter was sitting next to him. "For the most important calls," we're told, "reach out."

The Tribal Drum

The ad from AT&T shows us the great gift of cell phones. It's true that they can keep us more connected when we're in far-off places. However, the ability to connect from far away didn't originate with the cell phone, but with a series of inventions between 1850 and 1890 that harnessed the power of electricity. They completely dissolved and then reconstituted the communication structure in the West. One of them — the radio — used waves in the air instead of wires on the land to communicate. Oddly enough, this can be seen as the father of the cell phone. Just like cell phones, the radio allowed acoustic communication to take place across vast distances with little regard for the limitations of physical space.

When radio programs began broadcasting to a highly literate and individualistic culture, there was a reversal of sorts. The radio returned our culture to the experience of the tribal campfire with its shared stories, songs, and banter. Marshall McLuhan was among the first to recognize that the radio led to a retribalization of our culture, observing, "Radio provided the first massive experience of electronic implosion, that reversal of the entire direction and meaning of literate Western civilization."[1]

With radio we began to share simultaneous oral experiences on a scale never before known to human culture. You are reading this book on your own private time, but to participate in a radio event you listen in at the same moment as thousands or millions of others. You're connected to a much larger shared experience.

Television extended radio's power of group experience on a mass scale, helping to reverse the individualism of the print era. An individual is defined in part by a set of experiences unique to that person. An individual has a unique point of view, but that unique point of view disappears during a television program. Consider the tragedy of September 11, 2001. The millions of us who watched the catastrophic events on television witnessed the same event at the same moment from the same camera angles—this was a group experience on a global scale.

Over time we become accustomed to these sorts of group experiences. We start to feel connected with others who are watching the same program we are. We become a tribe across great distances and the individualism of the print age grows dim.

Cell Phone Kiss

During the AT&T wireless campaign, Nextel launched its own ad. It opened with a wide shot of a beautiful church with a wedding ceremony already in progress. A close-up revealed that the bride, groom, and priest are all holding cell phones in the walkie-talkie position, and the ceremony is performed with an efficiency that would leave NASCAR pit crews salivating. In the next ten seconds we hear the entire ceremony. A Nextel chirp precedes the priest's opening words:

Priest: "Mike. Sue."

Couple: "Yes."

Priest: "Love and honor?"

Couple: "Yes."

Priest: "Sickness, health?"

Couple: "Uh-huh."

Priest: "Objections?"

[*silence*]

Priest: "Rings?"

[*Bride and groom flash jazz-hands to show rings already on fingers.]*

Priest: [*to groom*] "Do you?"

Groom: "I do."

Priest: [*to bride*] "Do you?"

Bride: "I do."

Priest: "Kiss?"

[*Bride and groom make a kissing sound through their respective phones.*]

Priest: "Husband and wife."

[*Congregation cheers.*]

Priest: [*shouting*] "Next!"

The ad ends with the tag line, "Nextel. Done." The message of the ad is simple: Cell phones make you more efficient. Besides connecting us, efficiency is the other main reason people buy them. You get more done in less time. Yet every time I saw this ad, I gazed at the television with the curious head tilt of the RCA dog in front of the phonograph. An efficient wedding—what a strange thing to depict. Nextel, while attempting to highlight one benefit of cell phones, accidentally showcased an important truth: Cell phones often put artificial barriers between us and our loved ones. They separate us.

Taken together, these ads reveal the paradoxical effect of mobile technology on our culture. It has a remarkable capacity to bring those far away much closer (AT&T), while at the same time making those near us more distant (Nextel). There are two opposing forces at work in us: collision and division. Wireless technology is complex, contradictory, and deserves to be evaluated carefully.

The Tribe of Individuals

Perhaps I'm taking a couple of ads too seriously. Both are clearly exaggerations meant to entertain and sell. But the point is closer to home than many of us realize.

I have two friends who are best friends. Each was the best man in the other's wedding. They talk every day, sometimes more than once, on their cell phones. They live only a few blocks from each other. Yet recently, one told me that he hadn't *seen* his best friend in two months—two months! That's more than a hundred phone calls, and countless chances to hop in the car or walk a few blocks to see each other. Their friendship is withering from lack of true contact; each person has separately lamented to me that they don't feel they know the other person. Is it a stretch to think that the illusion of real contact provided by the cell phone has something to do with this sad story?

Electronic culture disembodies and separates us from those closest to us. Most of us are quite unaware of this phenomenon and, in fact, believe our technology is bringing us closer.

I was eating lunch with one of those friends when his phone rang and he answered it. He briefly apologized for the interruption and then joined his wireless conversation. In that moment, he was deported electronically, leaving me to dine by myself. At least I did have the pleasure of listening to *half* of a conversation — oh, and I also enjoyed *watching* him laugh at a joke that must have been quite funny.

The near become far, and the far are brought near.

This is the paradox of the electronic age. In this sense it retrieves and combines the characteristics of two previous media eras. If oral culture is tribal and literate culture is individual, the electronic age is essentially a tribe of individuals. This is a confused state of being in which we are thrown together from far-off places. We desire connection and community in our increasingly nomadic existence — yet we wander around the globe, glancing off other digital nomads without ever knowing or being known.

It is a condition we create with the smallest decisions. But it is just as easily undone. I was sitting with a different friend at lunch one day. His cell phone rang. I stopped talking and said, "You can get that, if you need to." Without blinking or checking the phone he said, "You took the time and effort to get together with me. Whoever is calling didn't. Now, what were you saying?" All he did was ignore his phone long enough to be present where his body was. Not only did I feel honored, but it also made me appreciate the gift of being there. Prioritizing those who are physically present can have a transforming effect on us when so many are digitally absent.

Empathy at a Distance

This unprecedented collision of two previous eras generates other paradoxes as well. If oral culture is intensely connected or empathic and print culture is distant or detached, then our electronic experience creates a kind of empathy at a distance.[2] This is what happens when famines, wars, and natural disasters halfway around the world flicker into our lives on our various screens. Our immediate response is often to give money, which is our way of extending compassion to far-off places. This response is good.

In the 1960s, the Civil Rights movement gained popular support in the North because television exposed the horror and injustice of white police officers pummeling with fire hoses the bodies of defenseless black citizens. The public's emotional outrage over this situation provided President Kennedy with the necessary mandate to take action. Television images were gas on the fire of the Civil Rights movement.

Televised disasters and injustices extend our feelings to those who are suffering around the globe. These feelings often prompt actions. Yet they are emotional actions, since television bypasses the intellect. Whatever action we do take is short-lived. This is a kind of self-protection, since we never know when the next earthquake, hurricane, or famine will fill our screens. So while our hearts go out to people suffering far away, the medium of television is also encouraging apathy and inaction. Like our self-image problems, though, this isn't our fault.

The human psyche isn't designed to withstand the full gravity of planetary suffering. Numbness and exhaustion are natural reactions. Feeling helpless and hopeless is nearly inevitable. The heart can only stretch so far so many times before it is worn thin and wrung dry. This is empathy at a distance.

Over time, if unchecked, this numbness undermines our ability to extend compassion to those in our own city, neighborhood, or even our own homes. The pain of the world, experienced through television, can keep us from understanding and alleviating the pain we encounter in our daily lives. The task of recalibrating our psyche and reigniting compassion must begin with local relationships.

I sat recently with a friend whose wife had left him. He wept bitterly as the shock and numbness began to wear off and deep grief emerged. I offered a glass of water, put my arm around him, and wept with him. Eventually, he talked and I listened. He had a lot to say, while I had nothing. By the end of the evening, we were utterly exhausted.

In the midst of this darkness, I did not feel hopeless or apathetic. If anything, I felt a renewed commitment to help any way I could. My response is hardly a reflection on what a good guy I am—it just shows that

I'm human. That's how we're made. When pain and suffering are right in front of us, we're moved to act and respond. Exposure to local traumas revitalizes our compassionate instincts.

Direct service to people around us heals our feelings of helplessness and apathy. It is quite possible that the needs in some far-off place are greater. But you aren't there. You're here, and there are needs galore in your own backyard. We do what we can, where we are, and watch the world change life by life.

Who do you know locally that is in need? Practice compassion with them and be made whole again.

CHAPTER 11

Our Nomadic Life

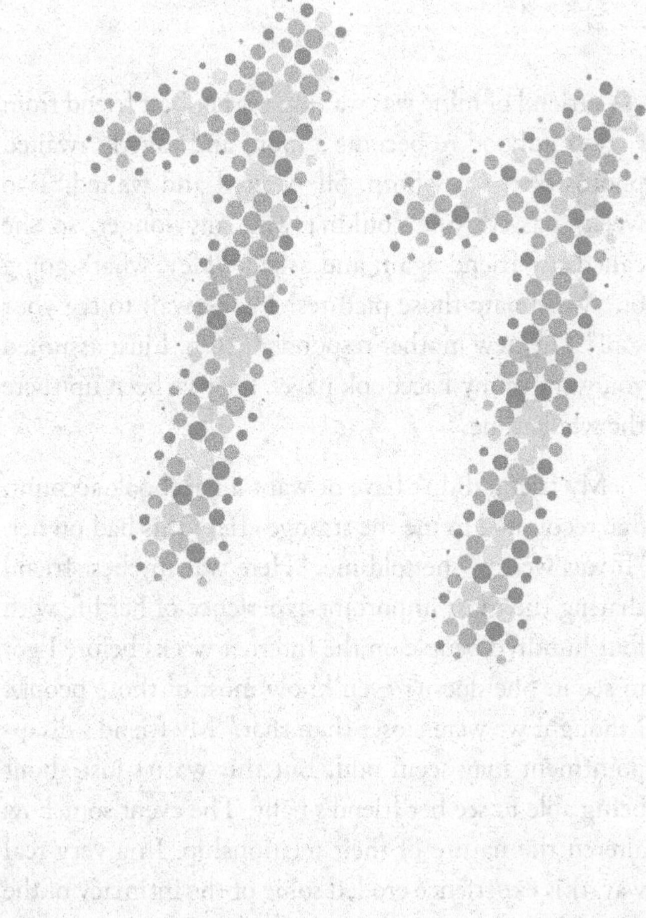

A friend of mine was waiting for her best friend from childhood to become a mom and eagerly awaited photos of the newborn. She waited and waited. Two weeks passed. She couldn't wait any longer, so she called her friend again and asked, "Hey, what's going on? Where are those pictures? I can't wait to see your son!" The new mother responded, "Oh, I just assumed you went to my Facebook page. They've been up there the whole time."

My friend didn't have or want a Facebook account. She recounted to me the strange effect this had on her. "It was weird," she told me. "Here was my best friend sharing the most important experience of her life with four hundred people on the Internet weeks before I got to see it. She doesn't even know most of those people. I thought we were closer than that." My friend's disappointment may seem odd. But this wasn't just about being able to see her friend's baby. The event somehow altered the nature of their relationship. In a very real way, this experience eroded some of the intimacy of the friendship.

Intimacy happens the moment we are invited into the exclusive VIP room of another person's life. Intimacy always follows the statement, "I'm going to tell you something I've never told anyone before." These are risky words of deep trust and vulnerability. The exclusivity of personal information creates the conditions of intimacy. That intimacy is preserved in that relationship as long as the information remains exclusive. The moment it is available to anyone and everyone is the moment intimacy begins to evaporate.

The Internet has a natural bias toward exhibitionism and thus the erosion of real intimacy. There is nothing exclusive about it, yet it creates, paradoxically, a kind of illusion of intimacy with people we've never met in person. This is the phenomenon of anonymous intimacy—the feeling of a relationship, but one that hasn't been, and likely never will be, face to face. The most immediate example of anonymous intimacy is Internet pornography, where extremely intimate visual and verbal information is shared between utter strangers. But this is only the most obvious example of the condition.

The less obvious version is the experience my friend had. In the moment she lost intimacy with her friend, something else was happening. Four hundred disembodied digital acquaintances (ironically called "friends," whether they were or not) experienced the honor of being ushered into the recovery room moments after the birth. Suddenly, we have the illusion of closeness with someone while remaining totally anonymous.

This anonymous intimacy has a strange effect. It

provides just enough connection to keep us from pursuing real intimacy. In a virtual community, our contacts involve very little real risk and demand even less of us personally. Vulnerability is optional. A community that promises freedom from rejection and makes authentic emotional investment optional can be extremely appealing, remarkably efficient, and a lot more convenient.

Virtual community is infinitely more virtual than it is communal. It's a bit like cotton candy: It goes down easy and satiates our immediate hunger, but it doesn't provide much in the way of sustainable nutrition. Not only that, but our appetite is spoiled. We no longer feel the need to participate in authentic community. Authentic community involves high degrees of intimacy, permanence, and proximity.[1] While relative intimacy can be gained in virtual settings, the experiences of permanence and proximity have all but vanished.

I'm not morally opposed to cotton candy *or* virtual community. However, I am concerned that virtual community is slowly becoming our preferred way of relating. I don't think the results will be any better than if we started eating spun sugar for breakfast, lunch, and dinner.

The Blogging Mind

Avid political blogger and *Atlantic Monthly* columnist Andrew Sullivan made this revealing observation in a post entitled "A Blog Sabbath?"

> I'm all but surgically attached to the web. I'm

> working 24/7, and increasingly isolated from social interaction. Going to the *Atlantic* offices helps, but getting a grip on this thing is hard. The blogging mind does not easily adjust to reading a book or allowing an unformed thought stay unformed. Even when you carve out time for more offline reading or living, it's hard to switch gears. And the danger of burnout is serious.[2]

Evidence of his addiction is found in the fact that his blog now serves as his confession booth. Only instead of a priest there to absolve him, there are a million disembodied, faceless, and anonymous avatars who offer their well-intentioned, but helpless and hollow, condolences.

I find it troubling that so many communities of faith are in hot pursuit of these technologies. The Internet is seen as the Holy Grail of "building community." However, churches will find the unintended consequences of this medium coming back to bite them. The Internet is a lot of things, but it is emphatically *not* a neutral aid. Digital social networking inoculates people against the desire to be *physically present* with others in real social networks—networks like a church or a meal at someone's home. Being together becomes nice but nonessential.

Our addiction to virtual community is understandable. The convenience factor is just too high. We love the efficiency of our interactions; they allow us to be in touch more often. However, there is a big difference between being "in touch" and truly connecting with others. I discovered this, strangely enough, during my time in the business world.

My job depended heavily upon people in several other departments scattered throughout the building. I was told that people in my role did their jobs primarily by shooting off emails to the relevant parties in other departments detailing requests and noting deadlines. Email, I was told, was a lifesaver; it was so much more efficient, and it was always better to have your requests down in writing.

I mirrored this method but found the responses to my requests to be slow in coming. Often, I had to physically track down the people and negotiate a solution to the problem. When I did, they would appear to be profoundly inconvenienced by my need for them to do their jobs. Judging from the lunchtime commiserating in my department, I wasn't the only one having this problem.

This was all happening at the same time I was learning how media and technology shape us. I decided to try an experiment. For two weeks, I only made my project requests in person. I took the time to track people down, sit in their offices, and carry on inefficient conversations about our weekend plans. Eventually, though, we would discuss my project needs. I found it difficult to find people, so I spent a lot of time prowling the hallways, and it was much less efficient than email.

However, something wonderful happened. As deadlines approached, people from other departments came to find *me* to deliver projects in person. This had never happened before. New project requests failed to generate the typical resistance. I also discovered that they worked on my projects before they worked on the email requests of my colleagues, even those with tighter deadlines. Our face-to-face meetings built relationships in a way email could not. These personal relationships made our working lives more enjoyable and, eventually, more efficient.

It turns out that professors at Stanford Business School performed a similar experiment on a large scale. They focused on business negotiations made face to face, over the telephone, and via email. They found that negotiations performed exclusively over email broke down far more often than face-to-face or even telephone negotiations.[3] The implications of these findings go far beyond business dealings.

E-Conflict

Not long ago, a friend of mine received an email from someone in the church he attends. Apparently, my friend had offended this person, and the result was a confrontational email. The email started out in a restrained manner, but soon devolved into personal attacks, unfair allegations, and comments easily read as veiled insults. The tone was curt, accusatory, and occasionally employed the dreaded ALL CAPS — a universal sign for yelling. My friend was deeply hurt by this email. Some of the accusations were utterly false; others were based on assigning motives my friend didn't have; all of them were conveyed with a lack of common courtesy.

My friend spent several days deciding how to respond. He wrote an equally involved email in response with a point-by-point refutation of the grievances, to which he added his own list of grievances. It was smart, controlled, and polite—but cutting. He asked me to look at it before he hit SEND.

His response was fair and certainly justified. But I had one concern: Why was he planning to email this friend rather than talk in person? My friend responded, "Well, I wanted to be sure that I communicated clearly. Writing my thoughts down helps me figure out exactly what I want to say. I'm not as quick on my feet."

His rationale is understandable. The problem is that email and other text-based e-communication are designed for efficiency and, therefore, severely truncated. Intonation, body language, context, the rules of civil discourse, and the opportunity for midstream clarification are all stripped away, despite our best efforts to create a never-ending stream of emoticons. Given the limitations of email, the chances of miscommunication are near certain.

Using email to mediate conflict is like baking a cake without a mixing bowl or an oven. The very ingredients that make reconciliation possible are absent. Reconciliation comes in the context of clear communication, meaningful listening, shared understandings, civility, openness, and a lot of patience. The medium of email inevitably removes these delicate ingredients.

My friend decided to respond to his accuser face-to-face. A few days later, I followed up and learned that my friend had misunderstood the email. The person was more confused than angry. In fact, the person apologized because he didn't realize how negatively his email was received.

This experience of e-conflict—whether via email, texting, MySpace, or blogs—is growing ever more common. Electronic text as a medium stunts our best efforts to resolve conflict. Countless hours and precious emotional energy are wasted combing over messages, parsing word choices, verb tenses, and leaps in logic. Even more time is wasted crafting the perfect digital response. And yet on nearly every occasion, such misunderstandings and hurt feelings can be avoided simply by speaking to each other directly.

Jesus understood this truth about conflict resolution. In the book of Matthew he tells his disciples, "If your brother sins against you, go and show him his fault, just between the two of you. If he listens to you, you have won your brother over."[4] The time-tested words of Jesus couldn't be more relevant to our digital culture. Perhaps if he were able to update this teaching for the digital age, he might add a new emphasis: "If your brother sins against you, *don't email him about it.* Instead, go directly to him."

Unfortunately, we seem to have a growing habit of throwing stones from a safe distance. And why not? Anonymous intimacy—and distant hostility—is not only possible, it's encouraged by our culture. And therein lies the problem.

The gospel is fundamentally about reconciliation. The best news imaginable in our broken world is the promise of broken relationships being restored. Jesus offers healing between God and his creation, peace between friends and enemies, and peace within. Yet often the only thing it takes to derail this wonderful, fragile process is a thoughtless email.

So delete that email draft you've been working on for three days and go find the person that offended you, or the friend you want to catch up with. I promise, it will make the world a more peaceful place.

CHAPTER 12

Next Door Enemy

In the 1960s, intentional communities started popping up all over America. Among other things, these communes wanted to recover the human experience of living life cooperatively and closely. They often shared their possessions and living spaces as well. Not coincidentally, these tribal experiments began shortly after the retribalizing medium of television had become a near-universal household appliance in the late 1950s.[1]

However, while efforts to build intentional communities have continued, it is estimated that nearly ninety percent of these communal experiments in North America fail.[2] I know people who enthusiastically entered into intentional communities and left shortly after to recover from what they described as emotionally invasive experiences. This doesn't mean healthy intentional communities are impossible; I also know many people for whom community living is preferred. My wife and I have lived intentionally with others and had positive experiences. But the failure rate should give us pause.

Part of the failure rate can be attributed to our diminished ability to handle interpersonal conflict. However, there is a more fundamental reason that life together is so difficult. Despite the retribalizing force of electronic media, our culture remains intensely individualistic. Electronic media have not done away with the individualizing forces of literacy entirely.

We are still a nation of readers. In 2007, 411,000 new books were published in America, selling more than 3 billion copies.[3] Consider the *Left Behind* series, which has sold an estimated 62 million copies, or the *Harry Potter* books, which have sold upward of 45 million. Even a nonfiction book like Rick Warren's *The Purpose Driven® Life* sold over 20 million copies.[4]

The age of print no longer reigns supreme, but we cannot chisel an epitaph on its tombstone just yet. The legacy is deeply embedded in us and not likely to die anytime soon. From its inception, America came into existence during the height of the print age. The First Amendment to the United States Constitution claims an inherent right to intellectual freedom, private judgment, and individuality. These values directly reflect the bias of the print mind.[5]

Our entire educational system is based on the mastery of reading and writing. As long as these educational objectives remain, individualism will continue to be woven into every fiber of our beings.

Beyond mere literacy, we have also developed a kind of digital nomadic existence—we are people whose electronic locations are in constant flux. Our nomadic life is a strange one. We do not sojourn as a group the way our ancestors did—we drift and journey alone. However, because we are constantly bumping up against digital avatars and acquaintances, we are hardly aware of our isolation. Electronic technology can fragment us even as we pursue connection.

Our deep individualism is partly to blame for the high failure rate of intentional communities and marriages, for that matter. A person so thoroughly shaped by individualism is simply not prepared to withstand the emotionally invasive experience of tribal living. Developing boundaries and having privacy aren't just something we prefer in this culture; they are integral to our emotional and psychological health.

In a purely tribal culture, identity is derived almost entirely from the complex interplay of relationships that comprise the tribe. The question of "Who am I apart from the community?" is almost never asked. In an individualistic culture, identity is determined in part by discovering the ways we are unique. We learn very early on to develop boundaries to mark the place where others end and we begin. We demand our privacy (which, thanks to printing, is our birthright in America) and seek to protect our personal spaces.

This creates difficulties for potential community groups in our culture. While the thought of community is appealing as an antidote to our often lonely and isolated lives, such community groups can also feel constricting and invasive. We need others to help us through the struggles of life, yet relationships we form present their own challenges.

What about the group member who talks too much

during meetings? Or the member who is too needy? Or the member I like but who seems to avoid me? These questions and anxieties weary us. It's easy for the group bonds to dissolve, freeing us once again to step into the fresh air of autonomous individualism. Somehow, though, we always seem to be looking for that idyllic community that will finally ease our loneliness and restore human contact. Maybe you can feel your own ambivalence about community? Are you aware of both an impulse toward it and an aversion to it? If so, that's normal. So, what next?

Neighbors and Enemies

We are thrown together and ripped apart by the tumultuous forces of our digital age. Into these push-and-pull conditions, the words of Jesus echo with greater volume than ever before. Of the many commands Jesus gave, two are of particular importance. First, Jesus tells a crowd gathered on a hillside to "Love your enemies and pray for those who persecute you."[6] Elsewhere, and much later in the book, he tells the Pharisees that the second greatest commandment is to "Love your neighbor as yourself."[7]

Perhaps the most powerful truth behind the two commands is that these two people groups—neighbors and enemies—are not all that different. In a world like ours, this distinction is blurred even further. The number of our neighbors is growing, whether digital or physical, and these neighbors have the potential to become our enemies. Cultural critic Andy Crouch puts it best when he writes, "No one gets out of any serious experiment in human community—church, marriage, family, or otherwise—without discovering, and becoming, an enemy."[8] This is an inevitable and uncomfortable consequence of living as the tribe of individuals.

Purely tribal cultures are accustomed to this conflict as a natural consequence of group relations, but for an individualistic and nomadic culture like ours, conflict feels unnatural and uncomfortable. Perhaps this is the reason we prefer to mediate our conflicts online rather than in person.

But if we are to take Jesus' words seriously, we need to develop better habits of interpersonal conflict. Even though face-to-face conflict is often avoided in individualistic cultures, that doesn't mean it goes away. Conflict simmers in the shadowy back alleys of relationships. Eventually, it will find more insidious ways to disrupt our lives if we don't keep it in the open.

Without a framework for healthy conflict, diagnosing problems—let alone solving them—becomes extremely difficult. When we learn to welcome conflict as a natural part of human community, we can dispel some of its destructive power. In fact, under the right circumstances, interpersonal conflict can be a powerful means of growth and intimacy.

There is one group of people that has best helped me understand healthy conflict—the Anabaptists. This 500-year-old stream of faith carries into our digital age a robust and practical theology of conflict.

Anabaptists have a long tradition of living in tightly

knit intentional communities. They have also chosen to take seriously Jesus' call to practice nonviolence. As a result, they have long struggled with what it means to deal with conflict peaceably. We have not always modeled it perfectly. We've had fits and starts, successes and failures. But I have learned that Anabaptists know better than most of us what it means to accept our enemies as our neighbors and live in peace.

Evidence of this can be found in a remarkable document of the Mennonite denomination, written as a voluntary covenant as part of a rule of life for local communities of faith. It's called simply "Agreeing and Disagreeing in Love."

Agreeing and Disagreeing in Love

Commitments for Mennonites in Times of Disagreement

"Making every effort to keep the unity of the Spirit through the bond of peace" (Ephesians 4:3), *as both individual members and the body of Christ, we pledge that we shall:*

In Thought

Accept conflict—acknowledge together that conflict is a normal part of our life in the church (Romans 14:1-8, 10-12, 17-19; 15:1-7).

Affirm hope—affirm that as God walks with us

in conflict, we can work through to growth (Ephesians 4:15-16).

Commit to prayer—admit our needs and commit ourselves to pray for a mutually satisfactory solution (no prayers for my success or for the other to change but to find a joint way) (James 5:16).

In Action

Go to the other . . .—go directly to those with whom we disagree; avoid behind-the-back criticism (Matthew 5:23-24; 18:15-20).

. . . in the spirit of humility—go in gentleness, patience, and humility. Place the problem between us at neither doorstep and own our part in the conflict instead of pointing out others' faults (Galatians 6:1-5).

Be quick to listen—listen carefully, summarize, and check out what is heard before responding. Seek as much to understand as to be understood (James 1:19; Proverbs 18:13).

Be slow to judge—suspend judgments, avoid labeling, end name-calling, discard threats, and act in a nondefensive, nonreactive way (Romans 2:1-4; Galatians 5:22-26).

Be willing to negotiate—work through the disagreements constructively, celebrate small agreements along the way, cooperate with the emerging agreement (Acts 15; Philippians 2:1-11).

In Life

Be steadfast in love—be firm in our commitment to seek a mutual solution; be stubborn in holding to our common foundation in Christ; be steadfast in love (Colossians 3:12-15).

Be open to mediation—be open to accept skilled help. If we cannot reach agreement among ourselves, we will use those with gifts and training in mediation in the larger church (Philippians 4:1-3).

Trust the community—we trust the community, and if we cannot reach agreement or experience reconciliation, we will turn the decision over to others in the congregation or from the broader church (Acts 15).

Be the body of Christ—believe in and rely on the solidarity of the body of Christ and its commitment to peace and justice, rather than resort to the courts of law (1 Corinthians 6:1-6).

Perhaps the most powerful part of this document is the first point: "Accept conflict." With this simple statement, we turn a potentially destructive force at work in our lives into a powerfully constructive one.

As theologian John Howard Yoder puts it, "To be

human is to be in conflict, to offend and to be offended. To be human in light of the gospel is to face conflict in redemptive dialogue."[9] Our task is to practice redemptive dialogue.

Very little of this approach to conflict resolution is new. In fact, the ideas are as old as Scripture. After accepting the inevitability of conflict, solving it is a relational process, and the process is all-important. Good process for resolving conflict cannot be underestimated. This is true on every level of human interaction, from the conflict between spouses to tribal or even international disputes.

The most effective method of conflict resolution always establishes clear rules and boundaries on process long before the content of a dispute is ever discussed. The process is almost always designed to help people gain distance from intense emotions, usually through structured listening and sharing, controlled feedback, and language coaching. When done well, the process will serve to de-escalate emotional tensions long enough to make space for rational dialogue, which greatly increases the chances of resolution. This is another way of saying that the medium *is* the message. The very *way* we disagree sends a message, and that process determines the *outcome* as much or more than the content of our disagreement.

To find our way into meaningful authentic community, more than anything we need a simple, robust, and practical theology of conflict. *How* we disagree matters more than *what* we disagree about.

CHAPTER 13

Getting Younger

On June 19, 2002, Hasan Elahi was detained by the FBI in the Detroit Airport on an inbound flight from the Netherlands. Elahi is a Bangladeshi-born American citizen, an artist, and a professor of media studies at Rutgers University. He had become a target of U.S. surveillance after September 11th and was under suspicion of hoarding explosives in a Florida storage unit. A lie detector test eventually confirmed his innocence.

Yet despite passing the lie detector test, Elahi's name is now one of the millions on the terrorist watch list. After this episode, Elahi did something unexpected. In an effort to avoid being detained again, he decided to call his local FBI field office to alert them of his future travel plans. He hasn't been picked up since. By giving the government coveted information, he seemingly took away their desire to know.

Going one step further, Elahi put his life online for anyone to see. His GPS location is available to you right now at www.trackingtransience.net. You can also browse through more than 30,000 pictures documenting what he ate or where he slept over the last several years. Elahi views information in economic terms—it is only valuable if no one else has it—so he has flooded the intelligence community with more information than it ever wanted.[1]

There is an elastic relationship between access to information and power. In the simplest terms, power is derived from information control. Whenever people have exclusive access to information, they are granted a certain degree of authority, which is why doctors, lawyers, and mechanics receive such deference. Who am I to argue when my auto mechanic tells me that the auger cap of my oscillator valve is cracked and it'll cost me $870 to fix? I generally defer to his authority and just assume I'm being ripped off.

As technologies cause information access to change, power structures change as well.[2] This has never been more pronounced than in the relationship between parents and their children.

Reverse Aging

In his short story "The Curious Case of Benjamin Button," F. Scott Fitzgerald tells of the birth of a child named Benjamin Button who, shockingly, appears in mind and body to be a seventy-year-old man. He is full-grown, gray-haired, and wrinkled. He possesses the wisdom, knowledge, and values of a man seasoned by threescore and ten years of life.

His parents, though struck with a mixture of dread and denial, soon learn to accept their son's condition. In time, however, they discover something even more shocking: Benjamin is aging in reverse. On his eighteenth birthday, he appears as a man in his fifties. He stands taller; his skin is smoother, his hair browner; his voice sheds its wavering cracks in favor of a stable baritone.

Years pass. Eventually, Benjamin marries and has children, who in turn have children of their own. But by the time he reaches his late sixties, Benjamin has the appearance and intellect of a toddler who is fast approaching infancy.

Most striking of all, Benjamin's own grandchildren have surpassed him in their knowledge and ability to navigate the world. They are promoted to kindergarten, while Benjamin is taken out of school altogether.

The story is fantasy, but the final turn in the story is an eerie parable of the age we live in. Most parents are enamored and terrified by the savvy with which their kids are able to navigate the latest technology. To many adult minds, the digital land is a foreign country with strange languages, norms, and practices. Parents are undocumented immigrants, while their kids are native citizens of the land and serve as interpreters and gatekeepers.

This shift marks the first time in the history of the world that parents have limited access to the world of teens and children. Go back five hundred years to the dawn of the print age and the situation was reversed. Printing empowered adults. It led to a more pronounced elevation of adults over children. It shrouded the adult world in mystery, leaving children on the outside straining to look in. A child wanting to access adult information was required to learn a complex code—phonetic literacy—which could take decades to master.

As a result, the print age dramatically extended the duration of this thing called "childhood." During the Middle Ages, a child became an adult as early as age seven—roughly the age he or she could contribute manual labor for the economic needs of the family. During the modern era, the goalposts were moved and adulthood was granted at the age of eighteen—roughly when the skills of reading and writing were responsibly internalized, at which point adolescents were able to access information in the adult world.

The electronic age changed all this by dissolving the information barriers of the print age. Radio and television don't have "access codes." These media communicate everything to everyone, and absolutely no skill is required to apprehend them. This means even very young children can have access to the same information that adults have. Broadcast media pulled back the curtain to reveal the mysteries of the adult world formerly hidden in the pages of books, and in so doing thoroughly changed parent/child power dynamics. Our age has seen the disappearance of childhood.[3]

As the digital age evolved, this dynamic continued to its logical end. The situation has now been inverted: Adults are disappearing, and children hold the power. Parents today strain for glimpses inside the mysterious world of their teenager's digital life. For the first time in history, teens are able to lock parents out of more than their rooms. It appears that adults are getting younger, just not in the way they hoped for.

The Digital Immigrant

Behold the mystery and wonder of the number 1337. It is the name given to a particular language that emerged with the advent of text messaging. Turn the number 1337 upside-down and it is the numeric equivalent of the word LEET, which is short for *elite.* If you're over the age of thirty, it probably seems elite. But for the millions of MySpace users, it is the common tongue. Nonetheless, those who learn it become like medieval scribes, hoarding scrolls containing sacred information.

The language was developed initially as a means of efficiency. It's just too cumbersome to text the full spelling of words. So abbreviations were developed. Simple examples of 1337 include:[4]

LOL = Laugh Out Loud

4RL? = For Real?

2L8 = Too Late

^5 = High Five

In time, however, another discovery was made. This language is basically an invisibility cloak to adult eyes. It became a deliberate teen encryption method. The more elaborate code looks something like this:

Teen 1: 411! F2T?

Teen 2: #-) but =W= 4U F2T

Teen 1: 420 4life & :-d~?

Teen 2: %\ & no cheddar

Teen 1: CD9 Lates

Translation:

Teen 1: I've got some information, are you free to talk?

Teen 2: I partied all night, but whatever, for you I'm free to talk.

Teen 1: I've got some marijuana; do you want to get high?

Teen 2: I have a hangover and I don't have any money.

Teen 1: Parents are around, I have to go, see you later.

The language lets teens convey devious and even profane messages while parents are reading right over their shoulders. The parent becomes Benjamin Button, an adult in body but with a toddler-like mind. Parents are reduced to the intellectual level of a young child who tries, mostly in vain, to decode the meaning of the squiggly shapes.

This is the great reversal of the digital age. The parent has become the child. This alters cultural values, norms, and expectations. Perhaps the most alarming consequence is that young people are granted startling and unprecedented freedom. Like the wayward kid whose parents are always out of town, the digital space is a land without supervision. When the parents become the children, they have little ability to provide oversight, boundaries, or direction to their kids. This is not trivial.

Establishing boundaries is of paramount importance to the development of young people. Boundaries are a powerful expression of parental love and protection. Without them, kids experience unconscious anxiety and insecurity. Eventually, they will go looking for boundaries. They will push, prod, and test limits in search of love and protection. When they fail to experience boundaries, security begins to fade. When emotional security is compromised, development actually stalls. And if development stalls, we will begin to see adolescence extend well into adulthood and, in some cases, indefinitely.

Establishing technology boundaries is not easy. For one thing, our kids will always know more than us. But the greater challenge comes from parents' best intentions. Parents may fear their kids will be left out or left behind if they restrict access to technology. Parents want their children to become familiar with the digital world so they'll be prepared to navigate it and succeed in this life. Parents realize that their kids connect with friends increasingly through digital means, and they don't want their kids left out of the tribe.

I'm sympathetic to these concerns, but there is flaw in this logic. In many ways our kids don't need our help with technology. They are digital natives; this is the air they breathe, it's all around them. My two-year-old already knows how to use a mouse. Our kids will figure technology out intuitively, just like the rest of us did.

On the issue of being left out socially, we should remember that digital space is the most anemic form of social interaction available. It is severely truncated, unsupervised, and easily addictive. During the most crucial stage of social and emotional development, maybe being left out of this is a good thing.

Regardless of how people choose to set boundaries in their own families, one thing is clear: This unprecedented empowerment of youth, along with our image-fueled obsession with beauty, is a dangerous cocktail. In a culture that worships youth, what incentive do our kids have to ever grow up?

CHAPTER 14

The Prodigal Brain

There was once a rich man who had two sons. The younger went to his father and asked for his inheritance. The father obliged, and the son left home and traveled to a distant country. There he squandered everything. One day, as he scrounged for food among pigs, he realized that even his father's *servants* fared better. So he returned home and begged his father to accept him back — not as a son, but a servant. However, the father immediately forgave him and prepared a sumptuous banquet in celebration of his son's return.

Meanwhile, the elder brother who remained home was upset. He had done the right thing, but he received no such celebration. His father said, "My son, you are with me always, and all I have is yours. But it was only right we should celebrate and rejoice, because your brother here was dead and has come to life; he was lost and is found."

Jesus tells this parable in Luke 15 to illustrate, among other things, the joy God feels when his children return to him. But the parable could also be a metaphor for the story of our brain in the last 500 years. Our brain is split into two hemispheres—the right-brain and the left-brain—which perform different functions. During the print age, the right-brain disappeared, like the younger son, while the left-brain stayed home.

As a kid I spent a lot of time being tested for learning disabilities. I didn't read much due to dyslexia. As a result, the left hemisphere of my brain was underdeveloped. I struggled with tracking sequences, creating order, and reasoning. When I grew older, however, I became a more proficient reader, and as a result I began to exhibit the skills of the left-brain. I became a different kind of thinker.

The printing press had a similar affect on our culture as a whole. Printing put the left hemisphere of the brain on steroids. The print age pumped up the muscles of critical reasoning, logic, order, and abstract thinking. The rules of logic that govern the printed word are neither intuitive nor innate to us; they require learning. It takes years to build up the intellectual capacity and patience necessary to understand arguments, unpack rhetoric, test "truth claims," debate meanings, and refute or appreciate conclusions. This is heavy lifting and requires the same rigors demanded of bodybuilding. These capacities require mentoring, discipline, and extensive repetition. The print age demanded the development and exercise of these left-brain skills.

Immediately following the introduction of the printing press, something unusual happened: nothing.

From the fifteenth century until the early nineteenth century, no new communication technologies were introduced to alter the way information was carried. As a result, Western culture had more than 400 years to get accustomed to the printed word.[1] By the seventeenth century, printing had become the dominant means of communication. And the left-brain became the dominant hemisphere of Western culture. It created supreme talents in the areas of science and reason. In time, these muscles grew out of proportion in the West. A tyranny of the left-brain was the unintended consequence. In the process, the right-brain departed for distant lands and was left to eat with the pigs.

The invention of the photograph changed all that. Image culture eroded our dependence upon printing. With icons displacing the dominant medium of text, the right-brain became the prodigal hemisphere, returning to a feast of images.

Images aren't the only thing in electronic culture that fuels the right-brain. The digital age has transformed the meaning of literacy. We still rely heavily on text, but the text-based communication of the Internet and instant messaging generate a fundamentally different kind of literacy—an unusual right-brained sort of literacy. With blogs, email, and texting, we may actually read more today than ever. However, the *way* we read has radically changed.[2]

Digital text and the printed book require very different energies and create separate muscles in the mind. Most books present an extensive, in-depth monologue, a thorough argument carefully crafted in linear, successive paragraphs and pages. This is true of both novels and nonfiction. The left-brain is heavily engaged by such activity. But Internet text presents a nonlinear web of interconnected pages and a vast mosaic of hyperlinks with no fundamental beginning, middle, or end. We are immersed in a boundless, endless data space. These are the conditions specially suited to the right-brain.

Like the father in the parable, we have reason to celebrate the return of the prodigal brain. The right-brain offers powerful gifts that went out of favor in the print age. The power of intuition, emotion, holistic perception, and pattern recognition are all gifts of the right-brain. The right-brain is the hemisphere that allows us entry into spiritual practices like contemplation, centering prayer, and silence. The left-brain is allergic to such practices; it is the dogmatic theologian rather than the intuitive mystic. It is appropriate to respond with the same enthusiasm as the father in our story and welcome the right-brain home.

The Disappearing Bible

While the father was filled with joy upon the younger son's return, the older brother did not share in his enthusiasm. He was suspicious and envious. In the same way, the return of the right-brain may concern us. The problem is not the return itself, but rather the way it is returning. The right-brain is barging back in like it owns the place. In fact, we may be at risk of exchanging one tyranny for another. Electronic media not only nurture the right-brain; it can even suspend activity in the left-brain.

The Internet is stunningly effective at enticing us to

open a Pandora's Box of perpetual links, sights, sounds, people, places, feelings, and ideas. Our intellects are spread a mile wide and an inch deep.

Consider blogs. Their great wonder is their dynamic speed. We are exposed to many more ideas than previously possible and given a chance to dialogue in near real-time. Yet because of their brevity and the constant evolution of content, blogs are forced to stay on the surface. Blogs are ill-suited for deep-level analysis and thoughtful reasoning. The Internet makes a flat stone of the mind and skips it across the surface of the world's information ocean. A book, by contrast, is a sturdy submarine, diving the mind deep into the sea.[3]

If you've made it this far in the book, your ears should be popping.

The emerging right-brain culture presents other challenges as well. Protestant Christianity is a by-product of a single medium — the printed Bible. Without printing, no one could have challenged the authority of the pope. How disconcerting to have a faith yoked so closely to a medium that is now in the dusk of its life, at least its life as we currently know it. Our culture has a shrinking preference — and even aptitude — for reading books, especially complex ones. If the Bible is anything, it is complex, so it should not surprise us to see a growing biblical illiteracy in the electronic age.

The Bible is an extraordinarily demanding library of books. The stories, letters, and laws are shrouded by the fog of time. The thick dusty languages of ancient Greek and Hebrew convey the message through cumbersome translations. The books were born in civilizations and cultures alien to us, and the assumptions and attitudes of the original authors often escape us entirely. In many cases, excavating meaning requires the fortitude, patience, and discipline of an archaeological dig.

In other words, bulging left-brain muscles are an essential tool for understanding the Bible. Unfortunately, our digital diet sedates the left-brain, leaving it in a state of hypnotic stupor. The left-brain begins acting like our great Uncle Jerry nodding off in the recliner after Thanksgiving dinner. Large portions of the Bible are growing faint and becoming inaccessible to the lethargic left-brain.

Brain Balance

One morning in December of 1996, a blood vessel burst in Jill Bolte Taylor's brain. She was a Harvard-trained neuroscientist who had spent her career mapping the micro circuitry of the brain in people with mental illness. That morning, over the course of four hours, she lost her ability to walk, talk, read, write, or recall any of her life.

The stroke happened in the left hemisphere of her brain, which is responsible for all the functions she lost. With her left-brain muted, over the next few hours she began to experience life through her right-brain only. She describes it as a vastly expanded state of consciousness; she was fully immersed in the present moment. There was no past or future, only the now. She lost her ability to perceive the boundaries of her body and became aware of her total oneness with the energy of the entire universe. Molecules of her body mingled with the molecules of the air and objects around her. Her subjective experience was one of extraordinary peace and euphoric bliss. Not a religious person, she called that place "nirvana" or, more affectionately, "La La Land."

It took a major surgery to save her life and two weeks to regain some measure of left-brain functioning. It took a full eight years to recover completely. But when she awoke, this left-brain scientist realized the incalculable value of the right hemisphere of the brain. Once her left-brain functioning returned, she learned how to establish a remarkable ecology or equilibrium between the hemispheres of her brain, which unleashed a torrent of creative and spiritual energy that had been dormant under the blanket of left-brain thinking alone. This changed her life completely. She later observed that this experience taught her more about the brain and human potential than all of her years of research.[4]

Jill Bolte Taylor's experience is an extremely rare case study that demonstrates the extraordinary potential unleashed in a person who establishes brain balance or whole-brain thinking.

My experience is far less dramatic, but equally telling. When I arrived at college orientation, I met with the school's learning disabilities specialist. I was terrified. I was barely a C student in high school, so how could I possibly survive the rigors of higher education? The writing was on the wall, and I was pretty sure it spelled *doom*—either that, or *mood.*

I sat in a small gray cubicle as the specialist reviewed the assessment results from my senior year of high school. She sat back with a big smile on her face. "Oh, Shane, your higher order thinking skills are intact. In fact, you have advanced crystallized thinking skills. You're going to do just fine here."

I didn't know what that meant, but it was quite a relief. I learned later that my particular way of thinking resulted from the interplay of the right-brain and the left-brain. Apparently, this kind of thinking is not uncommon among dyslexic people when the left-hemisphere is delayed in its development, but eventually catches up. Early in life, I was primarily a right-brain thinker. This is the hemisphere that uses the skills of synthesis and making connections between things. As the left-hemisphere of my brain began to develop, it introduced the skills of linear deductive reasoning or analysis. The interplay of these two processes caused me to think differently.

In my first semester in college, I got straight A's. I was sure there was a mistake somewhere—I wasn't that smart. It turns out that my courses and subject areas catered to crystallized thinking. Apparently, I had a knack for that thanks to the right-brain dominance of my youth. However, my ability to succeed depended upon the use of both hemispheres. The left-brain was crucial in this. It is the voice and translator of the non-verbal right-brain. Without the active engagement of both hemispheres, I was unable to perform crystallized thinking.

In the story of the prodigal son, the father seeks a way for his sons to coexist. He must manage the tensions and disagreements between them. He gives each their place and their due. The same task might also be applied to our brains in the digital age. It requires the establishing of the unity of opposites. Recovering a natural ecology of the brain will better equip us to navigate the challenges of our brave new world.

Brain balance is born by restoring an intentional relationship to our technologies.

CHAPTER 15

A Mirror Dimly

When I was in school, the bully was woefully unimaginative, usually resorting to the yank-the-chair-away-before-you-sit-down prank. Still, his techniques were effective in getting the rest of us to laugh—we knew that if we didn't, we'd be next. Eventually, though, we were *all* next. When it was my turn, everyone laughed, just like I'd laughed at them. All of us, except the bully, were caught in a trap with no obvious way out.

Discovering the hidden way technology shapes us is a bit like being the victim of a prank: We feel humiliated and trapped. When I first began studying media influence, I felt like the fish oblivious to the hook inside the worm. Fortunately, however, nothing is inevitable. There is not some predetermined and unstoppable effect of all media. In fact, the chair will continue to be pulled out from under us only if we remain unthinking. Our lack of awareness is what empowers the media to bully us.

This fact was not lost on Jesus. He sought to awaken us to this reality in the book of Matthew. In chapter

9, the followers of John the Baptist noticed something curious about the disciples of Jesus. They didn't fast the way everyone else did. When they asked Jesus why, Jesus told them that people don't fast at a wedding when the groom is present. It's a strange answer, so Jesus added an object lesson: "No one sews a patch of unshrunk cloth on an old garment, for the patch will pull away from the garment, making the tear worse. Neither do men pour new wine into old wineskins. If they do, the skins will burst, the wine will run out, and the wineskins will be ruined. No, they pour new wine into new wineskins, and both are preserved."[1]

Jesus understood the intimate connection between the methods and message, the container and the content. He tells us a new container (wineskin) must bear with it new content (wine); so also old methods (worn garments) will retain an old message (worn patch). Fasting was an important method for the Judaism of his day, and Jesus played with the method by telling his disciples to practice it in a different way. In this way, Jesus used a method to point to a new message. He pointed to a fresh gesture of God—not only new methods, but also a new message.

This object lesson has long been used to argue that our wineskins (our methods and media) must be constantly renewed and updated to stay relevant. But we may have missed the most dramatic point of this passage: The emphasis for Jesus is that the *wine* itself is new. Jesus came embodying a new message, not just new methods. For him, the two are inseparable.

Our methods and our message *must* both evolve.

While this may sound odd, it is actually a consistent practice of God. Throughout Scripture, God makes changes to his unchanging message. God promised Moses that he would give his people a land flowing with milk and honey. That is one message. Later God sent prophets warning of judgment, doom, and deportation if Israel didn't repent of its injustice and disobedience. That represents a shift in message, from the promise of blessing to the warning of judgment. From the perspective of ancient Israel those are two very different messages.

The mission of Jesus was executed largely in secret and focused almost exclusively on the Jews. At one point, he expressly forbids mission to the non-Jewish people.[2] In contrast, Paul's mission focused mostly on the Gentiles. Given these distinct audiences, we see in Paul and Jesus distinct messages tailored to each audience.

It is the difference between good news for this life and good news for the next. While Jesus and Paul represent both aspects, their emphasis varies considerably. Jesus focused on the good news of the kingdom of God at hand. A kingdom where the lame walk, the blind see, demons are cast out, and the captives are set free. It is a gospel located squarely in this world, even as it flows into the future and coming kingdom. But the gospel according to Paul had a different emphasis. For him, the good news was more often that Jesus Christ died for our sins and offers salvation for those who believe in him. It is a gospel that points us to the hope of the next life, even as it makes demands of us in this one.

A message that changes and evolves doesn't have to be contradictory. These messages are not inconsistent or irreconcilable. On the contrary, they are each acts in an unfolding divine drama in which God is reconciling the world to himself. The gospel message is not a single abstract concept. It is a story that changes and expands with each new set of characters and settings.

Just as in Scripture, this amazing story continues to develop today in new ways. With each turn in the story of humanity, we are introduced to new emphases as well as to potential limits on our understanding of the gospel. As we have seen, the print age led to an efficient gospel. Salvation became as easy as 1-2-3: (1) believe in Jesus; (2) apologize for your sins; (3) go to heaven. We were shown the power of a personal relationship with Jesus. The heavily intellectual emphasis of the print age helped unlock the treasure chest of Paul's rich, rational, and nuanced theology.

The image gospel is now moving beyond cognitive propositions and linear formulas to embrace the power of story and intuition. The rough-and-tumble story of Jesus recaptures our imaginations. We move from understanding salvation as a light switch to seeing it as a gradual illumination. We recover the conviction to follow Jesus in every aspect of life rather than merely with the mind. The gospel is seen as a way of life that transforms the world here and now, not just in the next life.

Different cultural conditions shape the gospel. In Latin America, the gospel of Christ is understood largely as the promise of liberation from very real and very evil sociopolitical oppression. The ministry of Jesus and the message of God's kingdom correspond to the Exodus event in which God freed the Israelites from slavery. In North America, however, the gospel is understood primarily as forgiveness of personal sin and the promise of eternal life.

Each of these views—and there are many others as well—presents a distinctly different message. They are inextricably linked to the particular social context from which they emerge. In a wealthy suburb of North America, the promise of liberation from political oppression has little meaning, while the assurance that one's personal sins are forgiven may provide little comfort amid the life-threatening oppression of corrupt dictatorships in Latin America.

When we claim the gospel message is unchanging, we risk boasting a kind of omniscience in which we presume to know the totality of God's mysteries and intentions. We presume to have discovered *the* one simple and unchanging message for all times and places, as if we somehow represent all of humanity past, present, and future. In the process, the Holy Spirit is made irrelevant and obsolete.

In the gospel of John, after a lengthy teaching to his disciples, Jesus said, "All this I have spoken while still with you. But the Counselor, the Holy Spirit, whom the Father will send in my name, will teach you all things and will remind you of everything I have said to you."[3] These words of comfort tell us two very important truths. First, when Jesus says the Spirit will teach you "all things" that means there is more to come, more that Jesus didn't say, more insights, expanded knowledge, deeper realities. Jesus is pointing us to a God who keeps communicating an ever-evolving message. That is why the Spirit is given.

Second, when Jesus says the Spirit will "remind you of everything I have said to you" it means what Jesus said back then is still valid. In other words, the teachings that went before aren't nullified by the new. The old should be included or integrated into our expanded understanding. It may mean the old is understood in new ways, but it does not make it void, irrelevant, or untrue.

I Could Be Wrong

Paul, a member of my congregation, was twenty-one when he was drafted. He was raised a Mennonite and learned to take the words of Jesus seriously. Paul was taught that when Jesus said, "turn the other cheek," "love your enemies," and "blessed are the peacemakers," they weren't just suggestions. As a pacifist, he made the unpopular decision to register as a Conscientious Objector during World War II. Immediately, he was branded as deeply unpatriotic and a coward.

The Constitution protected his right not to bear arms, but the draft still meant he had to serve. Paul was sent into alternative service at a mental hospital in Rhode Island. At that time, the word "hospital" was a euphemism for facilities that were essentially warehouses for the insane. Patient treatment consisted of beatings, straitjackets, and solitary confinement. They were crowded into large concrete gymnasiums covered by a sea of cots. They were neglected and often left unattended without clothing or in constraints. The inhumane conditions stripped the patients of dignity.

Paul became an orderly, along with a number of other young Mennonite men right off the farm. He was sent to serve in what was aptly named the "Violent Ward." It was no coincidence that young men committed to nonviolence were placed among the most violent and dangerous "patients." This was a form of retaliation for their convictions.

The patients lived up to their reputation. Paul was given ample opportunity to live the words of Jesus. He endured harsh blows, bruises, and even broken bones. They spit on him and called him names, yet he didn't retaliate. Instead, he and the other orderlies found creative ways to de-escalate the patients through nonviolent means. In the process, they inadvertently began transforming the state of mental health in America.[4] A philosophy known as "gentle teaching" emerged based on these results. It has been shown over time to be an effective and more humane means of behavior modification.[5]

Today, Paul is eighty-six years old. He shared his story with our community one Sunday morning, and after he finished I asked him why he chose nonviolence. Why didn't he just go into the Army? And why didn't he use physical force to restrain the inmates?

He paused.

"Well," he said, "Jesus taught us to turn the other

cheek. Jesus was nonviolent. And my best understanding is that I'm supposed to imitate that. So that's what I did."

He paused again.

"But . . . I could be wrong."

His words left me speechless. *I could be wrong.* Paul approached that life-changing decision with a humility that doesn't compute. Paul's steadfast commitment to his beliefs made him the object of physical abuse, humiliation, and threats on his life, all for the sake of following Jesus. People like Paul have earned the right to demand more from the rest of us. They have a right to call us to account. But he didn't. He finished describing his radical commitment with self-deprecating humility. *I could be wrong.*

Paul demonstrates the most stunning tension in the life of faith. His life and words reveal two things that seem contradictory in our world. He has found a way to hold two opposing ends of a magnet together — radical, life-threatening convictions and openhanded generosity for the beliefs and lives of others.

Paul demonstrates this strange yet potent cocktail of *daring humility.*

He practices his commitment to nonviolence even in the way he holds the belief. He is personally committed, but he refuses to coerce others to do the same. He won't demand that others agree with him. He just lives it.

Perhaps my friend Paul is simply wise enough to

see the truth of the Apostle Paul's words: "For now we see in a mirror dimly . . . Now I know in part."[6] We don't—and we can't—know everything, and the things we *do* know are unavoidably limited.

Certainty can be a great friend of arrogance.

My friend Paul and the Apostle Paul remind us that we live our lives with an open hand, acknowledging that we don't know it all. Such an admission rids us of the kind of certainty that leads to arrogance and even persecution of others. Instead, we are open to change and revelation as we grow into the True Vine who is never stagnant. Life is choked when we hold it with a clenched fist. It only flourishes when held with an open hand.

It's not that we can't know *anything*, just that we can't know *everything.*

Daring humility shuns boredom, complacency, and endless arguments. Daring humility is honest enough to admit that we see things in a mirror dimly, and bold enough to live a life of deep conviction anyway.

But I could be wrong.

CHAPTER 16

MediaGod

I've been a practicing Christian for over twenty years. My roots are in the evangelical tradition, but my journey has led me far and wide. In that time, I've heard a lot of sermons and attended countless Bible studies from a variety of perspectives and traditions. I learned a lot about what things are most important to God. In one setting, I learned that God cares most about saving souls and that he doesn't want me to drink, smoke, lust, or swear. Elsewhere, I learned that God mostly wants me to speak in tongues and be baptized by the Holy Spirit. A little further along, I discovered that the only thing God cares about is sociopolitical peace and justice. The list goes on.

I am certain that all of these things and more matter to God. But the one thing I never heard is that media and technology matter to God. Never happened. Not once. I suppose the most obvious reason for this is that God doesn't really talk about it much.

That may seem to be a reasonable explanation, except that it isn't true. In reality, God doesn't talk about it in the parts of the Bible we Christians like to read. There is, however, another part of the Bible, which tells a different story. Most of us don't notice this because we skip right over the passages where he talks about it.

In fairness, these are some of the most eye-blurringly tedious portions of Scripture. But it is here that you'll uncover God's deep concern over technology and its power to shape faith. The prohibition against the use of graven images was just the beginning. So gird up your loins and take a look at God's instructions to Moses on media usage:

> Make this tabernacle and all its furnishings exactly like the pattern I will show you. Have them make a chest of acacia wood — two-and-a-half cubits long, a cubit and a half wide, and a cubit and a half high. Overlay it with pure gold, both inside and out, and make a gold molding around it. Cast four gold rings for it and fasten them to its four feet, with two rings on one side and two rings on the other. Then make poles of acacia wood and overlay them with gold. Insert the poles into the rings on the sides of the chest to carry it. The poles are to remain in the rings of this ark; they are not to be removed. Then put in the ark the Testimony, which I will give you. Make an atonement cover of pure gold — two-and-a-half cubits long and a cubit and a half wide. And make two cherubim out of hammered gold at the ends of the cover. Make one cherub on one end and the second cherub on the other; make the cherubim of one piece with the cover, at the two ends. The cherubim are to have their wings spread upward, overshadowing the

cover with them. The cherubim are to face each other, looking toward the cover. Place the cover on top of the ark and put in the ark the Testimony, which I will give you."[1]

Devotional reading this is not—if you read the whole passage without skimming, you get extra credit. These are specific instructions for building the Ark of the Covenant—a medium intended to carry the presence of God on earth. You can see the special attention to detail God has for this container or medium, and this instruction manual paragraph is only the tip of the iceberg. Yahweh goes into excruciating detail for how to make and use all worship-related media and technology. In the book of Exodus, he describes every last material, dimension, design, and use for:

the Table for the Ark (25:23-30),
the Lampstand (25:31-40),
the Tabernacle (chapter 26),
the Altar of Burnt Offering (27:1-8),
the Courtyard (27:9-19),
the Priestly Garments (chapter 28),
the Altar of Incense (30:1-10),
the Atonement Money (30:11-16),
the Basin for Washing (30:17-21),
the Anointing Oil (30:22-33), and
even the Incense (30:34-38).

These are all media of one kind or another. It takes God over two hundred verses and six laborious chapters to detail the technologies to be used for worship

—and this is in a Bronze Age culture. How much more might God be concerned with our technology in the age of the iPhone?

The irony in all this is that while Moses was feverishly documenting all of Yahweh's technological commandments, the people of Israel started to fear that Moses—and God—had left them, so they decided to make a freelance worship technology of their own.

When the Golden Calf emerged from the mold, God was not amused.

Baby Drool

God is quite talkative, and he makes use of a wide array of media to convey his messages. But our God is also intentional about the way the medium and the message reflect and reinforce one another.

When God first speaks to Moses in the cave, he appears in the form of a burning bush. But it's a strange bush that is not consumed by the flames. The content of the message was, "Take off your sandals, for the place where you are standing is holy ground."[2] But the message of the medium was, *I am mystery, power, and Other.* A burning bush carries its own meaning, regardless of what is spoken through it.

The content of the stone tablets was the Ten Commandments, but the message of that medium is, *Don't take these lightly; they are binding and significant.* Imagine how differently the message would have been received if God had used skywriting on a windy day.

When the prophet Balaam strikes his donkey one too many times, Yahweh speaks through the animal. The words the donkey spoke were, "What have I done to you to make you beat me these three times?... Am I not your own donkey, which you have always ridden, to this day?"[3] God used the sentiment of the donkey to convey his own frustration with Balaam. The words were a rebuke and a challenge. But the medium of a talking ass was, well, funny or at least playful. God's a comedian. Few other mediums could adequately convey that blend of humiliation and humor.

This study could be traced through everything from scrolls, poets, prophets, angels, pillars of cloud and fire, and even the belly of a whale. Each medium carries with it a different force, and each conveys a slightly different message.

At some point in history, though, God decided that it was time to communicate with the greatest medium he would ever use.

A dazed, drooling infant in a manger—Jesus of Nazareth.

In Jesus Christ, God's medium and message are perfectly united.[4] As the opening of John's gospel tells us, "In the beginning ... the Word was with God, and the Word was God ... the Word became flesh and made his dwelling among us."[5] The most complete revelation of God to that point was expressed in Jesus.

It is a message that radiates from every part of his being. God emanates not only from Jesus' teachings, but also from his life. Even his birth proclaimed a message: *I am not a distant God high in heaven. I am a God who joins you, who experiences the hardships of this life, one who suffers with you. I am Compassion.*

His acts of healing spoke clearly: *I not only suffer with you, but I am a God who longs to ease, transform, and release you from your suffering.*

His longest teaching, the Sermon on the Mount, is not difficult to decode: *Love matters more than any other commandment. Love yourself, your neighbor, and even your enemies in the same way you love me. Ultimately, love has no opposite, no reversal.*

His death carried a message: *I live dangerously. Following me is not for the faint of heart. You will lose this world but gain your soul. Following me will cost some of you everything. But it will transform the world.*

His resurrection: *It's not so bad losing your life. Death isn't the true end—it's a birth into a world where every tear is wiped away. A new life where all suffering dissolves like a salt cube in the boundless sea of God's compassion, peace, and love.*

Jesus is God's perfect medium—and the medium *is* the message.

My Failed Attempt to Save Jesus

A while back I was talking with someone about his view of Christianity. It became clear he was quite hostile to the faith, in part because he had had some negative experiences with Christians. He shared several stories of terrible hypocrisy and arrogance in the lives of some believers, and as he spoke, I realized that I, too, had acted in similar ways more than once in my life.

In my evangelistic anxiety, I responded to his grievances with something like, "If you want to know what Christianity is really about, don't look at Christians. They're messed up like everybody else. Instead, you should look to the Bible and Jesus." It was a noble effort to try to rescue Jesus and the gospel by severing their ties with the church. Unfortunately, it was misguided.

After his resurrection, Jesus made a number of appearances. He returned to encourage his followers and urge them to spread his message. The book of Acts chronicles their efforts to keep this memory of Jesus alive by imitating him and helping others do the same. They organized themselves into various gatherings that met frequently to nurture the habits of Jesus. There is a letter addressed to one such gathering in the city of Corinth; in it Paul uses a metaphor to help them understand their identity. He tells them they are "the body of Christ."[6] The implication is that they are interconnected the same way a body is. But there is a much more stunning implication to this metaphor that is often overlooked.

If God's chosen medium for his message was the person of Jesus Christ, and the church is the body of Christ, that means God has chosen the church to extend his revelation in a special way. The church exists to embody and proclaim the good news of God's kingdom. If the medium is the message, the message of the gospel is conveyed by the medium of the church's life in the world.

You cannot separate the medium from the message. The church is simply an expression of the gospel. The church is a direct reflection of Jesus, God's chosen medium sent to *be*—not just to proclaim—a message of healing and hope to the world.

We are the message.

We are the message, in all our hypocrisy and fear, in all our giftedness and hope, in all our brokenness and bitterness, in all our faith and love, in all our gossip and self-righteousness, in all our grace and gratitude.

This is a great mystery.

Why would God choose such a frail, failing, and inconsistent medium to embody his abiding message?

Is it possible that God chose a collection of bent and bruised hearts to bear the message of redemption and reconciliation because that is a message in itself? Maybe God chose a medium of weakness to reveal his stunning power to reach through human failure, sin, and sadness to grow new life.

As often happens in my life, I wish I could go back in time and have that conversation with my friend again. My failed attempt to save Jesus from the church only served to intensify his antagonism. If I had another chance, I would lament with him and acknowledge the legitimacy of his frustration. I would say, "That sounds horrible. I can see why you find Christianity so off-putting. It makes me even sadder to think that I, too, have been one of those hypocrites. I'm sorry you had to experience that. By the way, you're right. We represent

Jesus. We should be better than that. Thank you for keeping us honest."

Fortunately, I've since had this opportunity with others. I've found my alternative response more often leads to important learning for both of us.

Whatever God's reasons for choosing the church to be the message, we should not confuse this idea with a demand for perfection. Our goal as a church is not perfection. Such a goal only breeds greater hypocrisy and broadens our blind spots. Instead we might seek, by God's grace, to become communities of humility, repentance, and authentic hope.

Humility comes when we see ourselves as beggars who have been gifted with food and invited to bring that food to others.

Repentance demands the courage to admit our weaknesses, acknowledge our wounding of others, and seek reconciliation.

Authenticity means that we bring our grievances with an honesty of emotion and openness to correction.

Hope means that in spite of the relentless terrors, tragedies, and traumas of life, we maintain a stubborn confidence that there is a greater story at work—a story that does not deny these painful realities but interprets them in light of the story's ending, an ending where weeping turns to laughter and despair becomes joy.

These community habits reflect the tenor and texture of the gospel.

By living them, *we* are the message.

CHAPTER 17

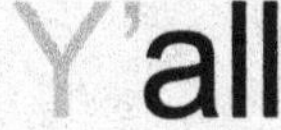

The sound of metal clanging on the pavement was ugly; I didn't want to see what had caused it.

The sight was worse than the sound. My wife, Andrea, was lying face down in a growing pool of blood, her legs tangled in the bike frame.

We were on our mountain bikes, traveling down a paved road with a slight downhill. For fun, I invited Andrea to draft behind me so we could pick up speed. As the hill started to level off, I slowed down a bit but neglected to warn Andrea. Her front wheel accidentally touched my back wheel, locked up, and she went down. Hard.

When I got to her she was conscious, but in a sea of scalding pain. It was like being thrown from a car going 30 miles an hour. An ambulance arrived soon after. With her vital signs intact, she was strapped to a gurney and taken to the hospital.

In the ER, the X-rays revealed that two bones in her

wrist had essentially turned to dust. Her helmet was destroyed, she had a hole in her upper lip, and a swollen face tattooed with road rash. A deep and gory puncture wound caused extensive bruising to her knee. It was a difficult recovery that left her with little mobility and a lot of pain for three weeks.

This happened just days before the biggest job interview of Andrea's life. We had just moved to Pasadena, California, a year before and had no family within a thousand miles. At the time, we'd been attending a small church for only a short while, yet they quickly organized three weeks of meals for us.

One of the volunteers who brought us a dinner was a twenty-year-old college student named Xaris, the Greek word for *grace.* That became more than just a name to us. When she arrived, she put the meal on the table and then started cleaning the kitchen. I'm pretty sure a Q-tip was involved from the spotless look of things after she was done.

A hot meal and a clean kitchen in the midst of the chaos and mess of our life meant everything.

Other members like Tyler made sure Andrea didn't miss her big job interview when I wasn't available to help. He picked her up at our house, drove her to the interview, and helped her into the building. He then waited outside until the interview was over and brought her back home. This outpouring of love and support felt undeserved—we had invested so little in the community. We hadn't *earned* anything from these people. And that was exactly the point.

In 1 Corinthians, Paul says that the church is the body of Christ.[1] He uses this metaphor to help illuminate the unique qualities of the church. A body is both diverse and interdependent. A body is a whole greater than the sum of its parts. Most importantly, a body is tactile. A body can touch. If the church is the body of Christ, it means we are the hands and feet of God. The church is the incarnation of Jesus in the world.

As a pastor, I get a chance to see the body of Jesus in action. I have seen it live and breathe, touch and heal. Rose is a retired teacher and longtime member of our community. For the last several years she chose to serve the church as a children's Sunday school teacher. Rose exudes a kind of radioactive love for children. When they leave her classroom, they are practically glowing.

Not long ago, we got some shocking news. Rose was diagnosed with breast cancer and doctors had removed one of the cancerous lymph nodes through surgery. Afterward, three separate doctors recommended a treatment plan that included surgery, radiation, and extensive chemotherapy. But for some reason, and this is unique to her, Rose did not feel at peace with any of these options. She instead felt an overwhelming call to forego medical intervention and pursue a nontraditional method of prayer and anointing.

In response, a group of people from the church gathered together several times to lay hands on her body, anoint her with oil, and pray for her healing just as Jesus did many times in his ministry. When she returned to her doctor about a month later, they discovered that she was completely clean of cancer. Her doctor had no way to account for it and was shocked that this could happen without any medical intervention.

I have other stories just like this, but these are dangerous to tell. The reason is because they inspire hope. Hope can be dangerous. Hope requires that we risk something. What happens if I have hope and healing doesn't come? What does it say about God or my faith if nothing happens? I don't want to look like a fool or be let down.

These are fair questions, as I have stories that end a different way too. Those times when we gathered to pray, lay hands on people, and pray some more, but no physical healing occurred. We've watched some people die in the process. But I've never, not once, had anyone say, "I wish you hadn't prayed for me." Or "I didn't like being touched." Or "I should have never had hope." Even in the case of those who are dying, there is deep gratitude for our presence. There is something powerful about the gathered community, the warmth of hands, and the communal cry for relief and restoration.

For Andrea and me, the church was the strong arm of God tending to our most basic needs. For Rose, the church was the hand of God extending healing energy.

The church is God's medium *and* message.

Staring at the Sun

If the church is one of God's primary mediums for his message, we should try to understand it. But the church is hard to describe. In some ways, it's like the sun. We can't look at it directly. The best way to locate the sun is by its relation to other things, like the shadow of a tree or the heat we feel on our backs. In the same way, the church is more easily described by its relationship to, and impact on, the world. The Bible never describes the church directly. Instead, metaphors are used to illustrate the relationship of the church to other things. These images help trace the contours of this mysterious medium.

The metaphors describing the church in the Bible are often overlooked. We can blame this on the limits of the English language, which is often less precise than Greek. For example, the word *you* in Greek can have different case endings that can change its meaning from singular to plural. In English, we're stuck with one word—*you*—that might mean one person and might mean a group. This is why Southerners invented the compound "y'all" to make it clear that a group is being addressed.

This little fact changes the way we read the Bible. It turns out the Bible was not written to individuals for their personal faith journeys. It was written to groups of people hoping to live as communities of faith. This is especially true of Paul's letters. Almost all of his letters are addressed to churches, not individuals. Paul is the master gardener of God's medium. His letters till the soil, pull weeds, and plant seeds. Paul's exhortations and encouragements serve as pruning and shade to help these communities become better God-carriers.

In 1 Corinthians Paul writes, "Do you not know

that your body is a temple of the Holy Spirit, who is in you, whom you have received from God? You are not your own; you were bought at a price. Therefore honor God with your body."[2]

For my entire Christian life, I had understood this passage as a call to personal purity and individual morality. I was taught that if I was ever tempted to drink, get a tattoo, or smoke, this verse could serve as a cocked and ready defense. While I am grateful it warded off certain temptations, Paul is not talking about individual purity. He is talking about the church.

Every time Paul says "you" in this passage it is plural, yet every time he says "body" it is singular. He is speaking to a corporate group about their shared body—the church. The *church* is the temple of the Holy Spirit, not me personally. Paul is emphasizing that the Spirit dwells in the corporate body. Our individual purity still matters, and the Bible still teaches that the Spirit dwells in us personally, but *this* passage is actually concerned with the church community as a whole.

Paul assumes that our personal faith journey is bound up and rooted in a larger community of people who serve together, not individually, as God's medium. This means the church does not exist only for us, we exist for it—each an essential part in the incarnated body of Jesus in the world.

Jim and Dianne are members of our church who lived in their home for thirty-seven years. One night Jim heard a strange noise outside. He went to check it out and saw a crowd gathered in the street watching his neighbor's house burn to the ground. It was a terrible sight. But as they waited for the fire department, the scene took another grim turn. The fire leapt onto Jim and Dianne's house. By the time the fire department arrived and the blaze was put out, nearly half of their home was reduced to black ash. And the other half, including all their possessions, sustained severe smoke and water damage. This disaster left them devastated and dazed.

The response by our church community was organic and immediate. Within hours a workday was organized. Nearly a hundred people arrived on the scene. Each person was invited to take several possessions from the house and bring them home. From there, they washed, cleaned, or repaired what they could and then stored them until Jim and Dianne found a more permanent home. In the meantime, a member of the church who worked at a retirement community found a vacant apartment and let them stay there until they figured out their next steps. Eventually, Jim and Dianne found another place to live, and the community began returning all the possessions that survived. Jim and Dianne were overwhelmed by the love and support.

This story shows us the corporate power of the community that Paul had in mind for the church. While many acts of kindness and hospitality can be performed by one or two people, this one required the work of an entire congregation. Many hands make light work. And this would not have been accomplished with two, three, or even five people. These things don't happen when we are lone rangers of faith. God was up to something when he decided to use a corporate medium as his message.

Salty Light

In the book of Matthew, Jesus says, "You are the salt of the earth . . ." and "You are the light of the world."[3] The metaphors of salt and light are often seen as a call to personal witnessing. The famous song lyrics tell it all: *This little light of mine, I'm gonna let it shine.*

But the song misses the communal quality of the metaphor. Once again, these images are addressed to and describe a group, not individuals. Like Paul, when Jesus says *you*, it's plural, while the word *light* is singular: *Y'all are the light of the world.* We are not a thousand points of light; we are a city on a hill. My little light means less to Jesus than our one big light.

The images of salt and light stress the reality that the church is present in the world and at the same time quite different from it. It is present and penetrating, but also a contrast from it.

In other words, we are strange, but not strangers.

Jesus goes on to tell us exactly what makes us strange. The rest of chapter 5 in Matthew begins the revolutionary Sermon on the Mount. This is a commentary on how to be salt and light. These are the practices of people who gather and live as God's medium.

Deal with disagreements directly, and practice reconciliation regularly (5:22-25). A wound becomes infected if not cleaned quickly.

Honor your agreements even when it's not fun (5:31-32). Otherwise, we become the purveyors of injustice and exploitation.

If you're the victim of injustice, expose it rather than return it (5:38-39). Escalation never ends well.

Be generous in the face of greed (5:40-42). It's a reminder to others that God shows abundance in a world of scarcity.

Love your enemies and pray for them (5:43-48). That probably means we shouldn't kill them.

There is a common thread that runs through these teachings: relationship. Jesus is teaching us how we should relate to one another. He shows us the things required of us to live as a community of salty light. More than this, we learn that the way we interact as communities of faith is the very thing that amplifies, inhibits, or obscures the gospel message itself.

By practicing these teachings together, we become a better carrier of God before the watching world.

Bend

I was ten when I met William Lo. My dad had returned home from one of his many business trips to China. William was his Chinese counterpart and a translator who had returned for a meeting. He became a friend of the family and stayed with us whenever he was in town. He was probably sixty, but he didn't look a day over forty.

I remember waking and looking out the window to see our Chinese friend in the backyard performing what looked like a slow-motion dance. He would sway and lean as though responding to the wind. His arms would trace delicate, controlled arcs through the air. I later learned he was a master of an ancient martial art called Tai Chi and had been performing this two-hour ritual every morning for the last four decades.

Every now and then, William would teach me a few simple techniques. Once, he invited me to push him as hard as I could. I backed up and ran straight at him, throwing all my strength into his chest, only to find myself face down on the ground behind him. It was as though I had traveled right through him. As I got up, he said, "Now I'm going to push you lightly. Try to resist me with all your strength." I stood my ground as he offered a gentle nudge. The next thing I knew, I was on the ground again. At this point he shared a secret: "When someone pushes you," he said, "do not resist the force, or it will overtake you. Instead, you must understand the force and cooperate with it. Only then will you disarm it."

That day I learned that what doesn't bend, breaks.

It was a remarkably effective technique that worked to disarm a schoolyard bully later that year. And William Lo's counsel is also wise advice as we try to embody God's message amidst the forces that shape us. Instead of simply resisting or caving in to cultural forces, we are invited to study and understand them. Only then will we learn to use them rather than be used by them.

It can be deeply disconcerting to discover the subliminal power of our creations to shape our minds, message, and faith so dramatically. I'm not fond of the thought that I might be unknowingly controlled or manipulated. When I first learned about the hidden power of technology, I often wondered why nobody ever warned me about this. I remember thinking, *If media inevitably shape us this much, what are we supposed to do? How are we supposed to respond?* It felt a bit like trying to stop the earth from spinning.

In my search for answers I stumbled upon another of Marshall McLuhan's many sayings. He wrote, "There is absolutely no inevitability as long as there is a willingness to contemplate what is happening."[1] In other words, by understanding the forces that shape us, no outcome is inevitable. Which is the point and purpose of this book: to make us aware. When we realize, for example, that digital space has the extraordinary ability to create vast superficial social networks, but is ill-suited for generating intimate and meaningful human connection, we may treat it more like dessert than the main course.

This invitation to awareness and contemplation echoes the wisdom of William Lo, reiterates the lesson of the wine and the wineskins, and confirms God's instructions to Moses.

Stay awake. Look beneath the surface of things. And learn to bend.

If we do this, things won't sneak up on us so easily. Media and technology have far less power to shape us when they are brought into the light and we understand them. Perhaps the thing that prevents understanding is premature judgment. We are too eager to assign a value to things; we want to call something "good" or "bad" long before we understand what it can do and undo. This is the enthusiastic but self-destructive approach of Mr. No-Depth Perception.

Restoring our depth perception will require a thorough rethinking of one of our most basic assumptions: "The methods change, but the message stays the same." By now we know the countless ways that statement falls short of the truth.

In the end, though, our technology isn't about hardware or software, bits or bytes, 1s or 0s. In reality, every technology is traceable to us. They are extensions of ourselves and amplified imitations of our humanness. And if we humans are created in the image of God, then they are also extensions of God—a highly communicative God. A God always seeking to convey an ever expanding and evolving message. A message that finds perfect expression in the person of Jesus, and eventually the body of Christ—the church.

Evan, a member of my community, taught me the true meaning of McLuhan's most famous saying. Evan was in his mid-eighties when his wife, Martha, died. After so many decades of life together, it left a void he could scarcely have anticipated or articulated. Many people responded with a flood of cards, condolences, and flowers. He was grateful for them all. But as we sat and he shared about his grief, he told one other story. A woman who lived in the same retirement community approached him one day and didn't say a word. She walked up to him and simply hugged him for a moment and walked away.

"Shane," he said, "that's when I got what you've been saying. The medium is the message. She didn't have to say a word, and it meant more than anything else."

May we learn to become the hands, feet, and heart of God in a broken world.

Go therefore, and *be* the message.

Notes

Introduction: Hidden Pixels

1. W. Terrence Gordon, *McLuhan for Beginners* (New York: Writers and Readers, 1997), 2.
2. Marshall McLuhan, *Understanding Media: The Extensions of Man* (Cambridge, MA: MIT Press, 1994), x.
3. Exodus 3; Exodus 20; Numbers 22:27-30; 1 Kings 19:11-15; 2 Kings 22:8-13; and John 8:6-7.

Chapter 1: Mr. No-Depth Perception

1. Exodus 20:4.
2. Plato and Walter Hamilton, *Phaedrus and the Seventh and Eighth Letters* (Harmondsworth: Penguin, 1973), 96.
3. Neil Postman, *Technopoly: The Surrender of Culture to Technology* (New York: Vintage Books, 1993), 5.
4. Postman, *Technopoly*, 5.

Chapter 2: The Magic Eye

1. McLuhan, *Understanding Media*, 18.
2. Marshall McLuhan, Eric McLuhan, and Frank Zingrone, *Essential McLuhan* (New York: Basic Books, 1995), 238.
3. See the Magic Eye website at http://www.magiceye.com/faq_example.htm.

Chapter 3: Stretch Armstrong

1. Marshall McLuhan and Eric McLuhan, *Laws of Media: The New Science* (University of Toronto Press: 1988), 98.

2. McLuhan, *Understanding Media*, 41.

3. For the original theoretical framework of this idea, see McLuhan, *Laws of Media,* 98. For a more accessible application to faith and culture, see my book *The Hidden Power of Electronic Culture* (Grand Rapids: Zondervan, 2005), 42, 60, 82.

Chapter 4: Dyslexia and Deception

1. McLuhan, *Understanding Media,* xxi.

2. The Greeks created their version of the phonetic alphabet around 700 BC and had mastered it by 400 BC. Like a slow gas leak lasting 1,000 years, the alphabet gradually infiltrated Western culture. However, this leak was all but turned off during the fourth century when papyrus supplies dried up, literacy rates plummeted, and Europe returned to a dominantly oral culture. In turn, the medieval Catholic Church began reflecting the characteristics of oral culture, leading to their increasingly mystical and sacramental theology. Literacy was reintroduced to the West in the twelfth century when Chinese traders brought paper to Europe.

3. Kenneth Scott Latourette, *The Chinese, Their History and Culture* (New York: Macmillan, 1964), 310.

4. Walter J. Ong, *Orality and Literacy: The Technologizing of the Word* (New York: Methuen, 1982), 87.

5. McLuhan, McLuhan, and Zingrone, *Essential McLuhan*, 244.

6. Changes in philosophy and religion have long been linked to the invention of the printing press and its role in the unprecedented distribution of new ideas to the masses. But it is rarely understood that these changes were caused more by the form of the printed word than by its content. In fact, the majority of ideas being disseminated in print were not new at all. In the 200 years following the introduction of the printing press, well over half of all printed books were medieval or ancient manuscripts. The public had a voracious appetite for classical thinkers. Even Martin Luther's ideas borrowed heavily from Augustine's fourth-century theology and

the ideas of the twelfth-century Waldensians. In spite of this recycling of medieval ideas, the form of communication during the age of printing caused the medieval worldview to dissipate and a modern worldview to emerge.

7. See Bill Bright's "The Four Spiritual Laws" on the Campus Crusade for Christ website at http://www.campuscrusade.com/fourlawseng2.htm.

Chapter 5: Subliminal Messages

1. Ong, *Orality and Literacy,* 78.
2. This calculation is based on the word count of Edwards' sermons, several of which were over 18,000 words long. A 30-minute sermon is typically only 2,000 words long.
3. George Whitefield, *Selected Sermons of George Whitefield* (Logos Research Systems, Inc., 1999).
4. F. L. Cross and Elizabeth A. Livingstone, *The Oxford Dictionary of the Christian Church* (New York: Oxford University Press, 1997), 532.

Chapter 6: Electric Faith

1. Neil Postman, *The Disappearance of Childhood* (New York: Vintage Books, 1994), 68.
2. McLuhan, *Understanding Media*, xxi.
3. Postman, *Technopoly*, 67.
4. Neil Postman, *Amusing Ourselves to Death: Public Discourse in the Age of Show Business* (New York: Penguin Books, 1986), 69.
5. Postman, *The Disappearance of Childhood*, 106.
6. Nicholas Carr, "Is Google Making Us Stupid?" *The Atlantic Monthly* (July/August 2008): 56-63.
7. John Borland, "See Who's Editing Wikipedia- Diebold, CIA, a Campaign," *Wired* (August 14, 2007): http://www.wired.com/politics/onlinerights/news/2007/08/wiki_tracker.
8. Plato and Walter Hamilton, *Phaedrus and the Seventh and Eighth Letters* (New York: Penguin, 1973), 96.

Chapter 7: A Thousand Feelings

1. Carl Erik Landhuis, et. al. "Does Childhood Television Viewing Lead to Attention Problems in Adolescence? Results from a Prospective Longitudinal Study," *Pediatrics,* vol. 120, no. 3 (September 2007): 532-37. See also Kamila B. Mistry, "Children's Television Exposure and Behavioral and Social Outcomes at 5.5 Years: Does Timing of Exposure Matter?" *Pediatrics,* vol. 120, No. 4 (October 2007): 762-69.
2. Denis Janz, *A Reformation Reader: Primary Texts with Introductions* (Minneapolis, MN: Fortress Press, 1999), 109.

Chapter 8: The Dimmer Switch

1. Romans 10:9.
2. Postman, *Amusing Ourselves to Death,* 72.
3. Mark 9:24.
4. Matthew 28:19.

Chapter 9: Soul Stealing

1. Daniel Boorstin, *The Image: A Guide to Pseudo-Events in America* (New York: Vintage Books, 1961), 57.
2. Lauren Collins, "Pixel Perfect," *The New Yorker* (May 12, 2008): 100.

Chapter 10: Together Apart

1. McLuhan, *Understanding Media,* 300.
2. Raymond Gozzi Jr., "Paradoxes of Electric Media," *EME,* vol. 3, no. 2 (2004): 127.

Chapter 11: Our Nomadic Life

1. Mark Lau Branson, "Forming God's People," *Congregations,* vol. 29 (Winter 2003): 22-27.
2. *Atlantic Monthly* columnist Andrew Sullivan made this revealing observation in a March 3, 2008, post entitled, "A Blog Sabbath?"

3. Sarah Smith, "E-Mail Etiquette," *Psychology Today* (July/August 2000): http://cms.psychologytoday.com/articles/pto-20000701-000009.html.
4. Matthew 18:15.

Chapter 12: Next Door Enemy

1. Joshua Meyrowitz, *No Sense of Place: The Impact of Electronic Media on Social Behavior* (New York: Oxford University Press, 1985), 133.
2. Dan Lazin, "Better Living: Too Many Social Experiments Start with the Best Intentions and End in Disaster," *This Magazine* (June 2003): 32-35.
3. "Unbound," *The Economist* (June 7, 2008): 77.
4. David J. Jefferson, "The Pop Prophets," *Newsweek* (May 24, 2004): 46.
5. Postman, *Technopoly*, 66.
6. Matthew 5:44.
7. Matthew 22:39.
8. Andy Crouch, "A Community of Foes," *Re:generation Quarterly*, vol. 7 (Winter 2001): 3.
9. John Howard Yoder, *Body Politics: Five Practices of the Christian Community Before the Watching World* (Scottsdale, PA: Herald Press, 1992), 61-71.

Chapter 13: Getting Younger

1. Clive Thompson, "The Visible Man: An FBI Target Puts His Whole Life Online," *Wired* (March 22, 2007): http://www.wired.com/techbiz/people/magazine/15-06/ps_transparency.
2. Meyrowitz, *No Sense of Place*, 64.
3. The observation and argument is further explored in Neil Postman's book *The Disappearance of Childhood*.
4. Candice M. Kelsey, *Generation MySpace: Helping Your Teen Survive Online Adolescence* (New York: Marlow, 2007).

Chapter 14: The Prodigal Brain

1. Postman, *The Disappearance of Childhood.*
2. Nicholas Carr, "Is Google Making Us Stupid?" *Atlantic Monthly* (July/August 2008): 58.
3. Some book publishers, in an effort to respond to the challenge posed by the Internet, have tried to mirror its form in books. They employ heavy-laden design elements and images, and margins embedded with critical comments or rejoinders by other authors. This is an understandable response to a threatening new medium. But the publishers misunderstand the power and purpose of a book. The form of a book is ill-suited to dynamic dialogue in the same way that blogs are ill-suited to express extensive, precise, and thorough analysis. To attempt either is like using a 747 to deliver mail between Dallas and Fort Worth. It is possible, but a gross misuse of the medium.
4. Jill Bolte Taylor, "My Stroke of Insight," *TED Online* (March 2008): http://www.ted.com/index.php/talks/jill_bolte_taylor_s_powerful_stroke_of_insight.html.

Chapter 15: A Mirror Dimly

1. Matthew 9:16-17.
2. Matthew 10:5.
3. John 14:25-26.
4. Albert Q. Maisel, "Bedlam 1946: Most US Mental Hospitals Are a Shame and a Disgrace," *Life* (May 6, 1946): 105.
5. For more information, see Gentle Teaching International at http://www.gentleteaching.com.
6. 1 Corinthians 13:12 (NASB).

Chapter 16: Media God

1. Exodus 25:9-21.
2. Exodus 3:5.
3. Numbers 22:28, 30.

4. Marshall McLuhan, Eric McLuhan, and Jacek Szlarek, *The Medium and the Light: Reflections on Religion* (New York: Stoddardt, 1999), 117.

5. John 1:1, 14.

6. 1 Corinthians 12:27.

Chapter 17: Y'all

1. 1 Corinthians 12:27.

2. 1 Corinthians 6:19-20.

3. Matthew 5:13-14.

Epilogue: Bend

1. Marshall McLuhan and Quentin Fiore, *The Medium Is the Message: An Inventory of Effects* (San Francisco, CA: Hard Wired, 1996), 25.

Resources

Boorstin, Daniel J. *The Image: A Guide to Pseudo-Events in America.* New York: Vintage Books, 1987.

Gordon, W. Terrence. *Marshall McLuhan: Escape into Understanding.* Toronto, Canada: Stoddart, 1997.

———. *McLuhan for Beginners.* New York: Writers and Readers, 1997.

Hipps, Shane. *The Hidden Power of Electronic Culture: How Media Shapes Faith, the Gospel, and Church.* Grand Rapids: Zondervan, 2006.

Janz, Denis. *A Reformation Reader: Primary Texts with Introductions.* Minneapolis, Minn.: Fortress Press, 1999.

Latourette, Kenneth Scott. *The Chinese, Their History and Culture.* New York: Macmillan, 1964.

Lohfink, Gerhard. *Jesus and Community: The Social Dimension of the Christian Faith.* Philadelphia: Fortress, 1984.

McLuhan, Marshall, David Carson, and Eric McLuhan. *The Book of Probes.* Corte Madera, Calif.: Ginko, 2003.

McLuhan, Marshall and Quentin Fiore. *The Medium Is the Massage: An Inventory of Effects.* San Francisco, Calif.: Hard Wired, 1996.

McLuhan, Marshall and Eric McLuhan. *Laws of Media: The New Science.* Toronto: University of Toronto Press, 1988.

McLuhan, Marshall and Lewis H. Laphan. *Understanding Media: The Extensions of Man.* Cambridge, Mass.: MIT Press, 1994.

McLuhan, Marshall, Eric McLuhan, and Jacek Szlarek. *The Medium and the Light: Reflections on Religion.* New York: Stoddart, 1999.

McLuhan, Marshall, Eric McLuhan, and Frank Zingrone. *Essential McLuhan.* New York: Basic Books, 1995.

Meyrowitz, Joshua. *No Sense of Place: The Impact of Electronic Media on Social Behavior.* New York: Oxford University Press, 1985.

Ong, Walter J. *Orality and Literacy: The Technologizing of the Word.* New York: Methuen, 1982.

Plato and Walter Hamilton. *Phaedrus and the Seventh and Eighth Letters.* New York: Penguin, 1973.

Postman, Neil. *Amusing Ourselves to Death: Public Discourse in the Age of Show Business.* New York: Penguin, 1986.

———. *The Disappearance of Childhood.* New York: Vintage Books, 1994.

———. *Technopoly: The Surrender of Culture to Technology.* New York: Vintage Books, 1993.

Yoder, John Howard. *Body Politics: Five Practices of the Christian Community Before the Watching World.* Scottsdale, Penn.: Herald Press, 1992.

Thanks

Writing a book is a solitary experience, but it is never accomplished alone. A lot of people are to blame for this book. I am grateful for all they've done, as it wouldn't have happened without them.

To Rob Bell: Thank you for pulling the pin. Nothing is the same.

To Zach Lind: For your friendship and relentless promotion of the ideas in this book.

To Gabe Lyons: For the megaphone you wield so generously.

To Tony Jones: For always pushing me to write more.

To Angela Scheff, my editor: For your incredible enthusiasm, advocacy, and stewardship of the creative vision.

To Chris Ferebee, my agent: For your time, industry wisdom, guidance, and stunning pursuit of such an unknown.

To Trinity Mennonite Church, my community of faith: For the chance to share my heart and words with you each week. You took a risk on me. I'm deeply grateful and profoundly honored. You have helped me become a better communicator, a better pastor, and a better person.

To my parents: For your relentless intellectual curiosity and a lifetime of love and support.

And most of all to my wife, Andrea: Thank you for radiating the deepest part of God's love. Thank you for never withholding your gift as a mother, wife, and friend. You are light, energy, and passion to me. Thank you for reading and wrestling with the ideas in this book and then pushing me further than I thought I could go. You ground me deeply and liberate me fully. I love you.

CPSIA information can be obtained
at www.ICGtesting.com
Printed in the USA
LVHW030353190820
663454LV00008B/286